Aleene's PRIZEWINNING CRAFTS

*From Readers and Viewers

Oxmoor House

Aleene's® Prizewinning Crafts from Readers and Viewers
©1996 by Oxmoor House, Inc.
Book Division of Southern Progress Corporation
P.O. Box 2463, Birmingham, Alabama 35201

Published by Oxmoor House, Inc., and Leisure Arts, Inc.

Library of Congress Card Catalog Number: 96-71091
Hardcover ISBN: 0-8487-1536-5
Softcover ISBN: 0-8487-1539-X
Manufactured in the United States of America
First Printing 1996

Aleene's® is a registered trademark of Artis, Inc.
Trademark Registration #1504878
Aleene's® is used by permission of Artis, Inc.

Editor-in-Chief: Nancy Fitzpatrick Wyatt
Senior Crafts Editor: Susan Ramey Cleveland
Senior Editor, Editorial Services: Olivia Kindig Wells
Art Director: James Boone

Aleene's® Prizewinning Crafts from Readers and Viewers

Editor: Catherine Corbett Fowler
Editorial Assistant: Barzella Estle
Copy Editor: L. Amanda Owens
Senior Photographer: John O'Hagan
Photo Stylist: Connie Formby
Assistant Art Director: Cynthia R. Cooper
Designer: Carol Damksy
Illustrator: Kelly Davis
Senior Production Designer: Larry Hunter
Publishing Systems Administrator: Rick Tucker
Production and Distribution Director: Phillip Lee
Associate Production Manager: Theresa L. Beste
Production Assistant: Valerie Heard

Front cover: Noah's Ark, page 6.
Back cover, top: Tacky Glue Mosaic Tray, page 14; middle: Corn Costume (left), page 76; Moravian Advent Star (center), page 106; Faux Stained-Glass Vest (right), page 58; bottom: Grocery Bag Valance, page 20.

Contents

Wonderful Wearables

Page 138

Page 35

Crafts for Kids

Holidays and Special Days

Product Information 144

Introducing the 1996 Crafter of the Year

Thanks to all of our readers and viewers! Without you, this book would not have been possible. To say that our first Crafter of the Year Contest was a success is an understatement! When presented with the challenge of creating and submitting designs in any of four categories (Crafty Home Decorating, Wonderful Wearables, Crafts for Kids, and Holidays and Special Days), you responded with great enthusiasm. We were overwhelmed by the more than 5,500 entries sent to us. We received submissions from almost every state and Canada. (The only state we did not hear from was Delaware. Come on, Delaware crafters. We want to see your handiwork, too!) Our judges were then faced with a challenge of their own. In only two months they had to select a first-place winner from each category, a winner for the best use of an Aleene's product, and a grand-prize winner who would be named our Crafter of the Year—as well as 45 honorable mentions.

Once all the judging was complete, we discovered that our big winner lived only a few hours away. We immediately thought how that gave us the perfect opportunity to surprise her by delivering the grand prize—a 1996 Geo Metro—to her in person. So on April 19 we drove to San Pedro, California, and surprised Georgia Skolil by naming her our 1996 Crafter of the Year!

This book features Georgia's grand-prize project along with all of the other prizewinning designs, for a total of more than 50 projects from 25 states and Canada. We think that you will thoroughly enjoy learning what your fellow crafters across the country are designing and that you will be inspired by their creativity.

Aleene

Tiffany

Tiffany and Aleene present Georgia Skolil with her grand prize: a 1996 Geo Metro.

Tiffany and Aleene discuss with their camera crew the best plan for capturing the big moment on tape.

Aleene informs a very surprised Georgia that she has been selected as the Crafter of the Year.

Tiffany, Aleene, and the camera crew edge up the sidewalk to Georgia's house.

Georgia takes Tiffany to her craft room to share her prizewinning project.

Noah's Ark

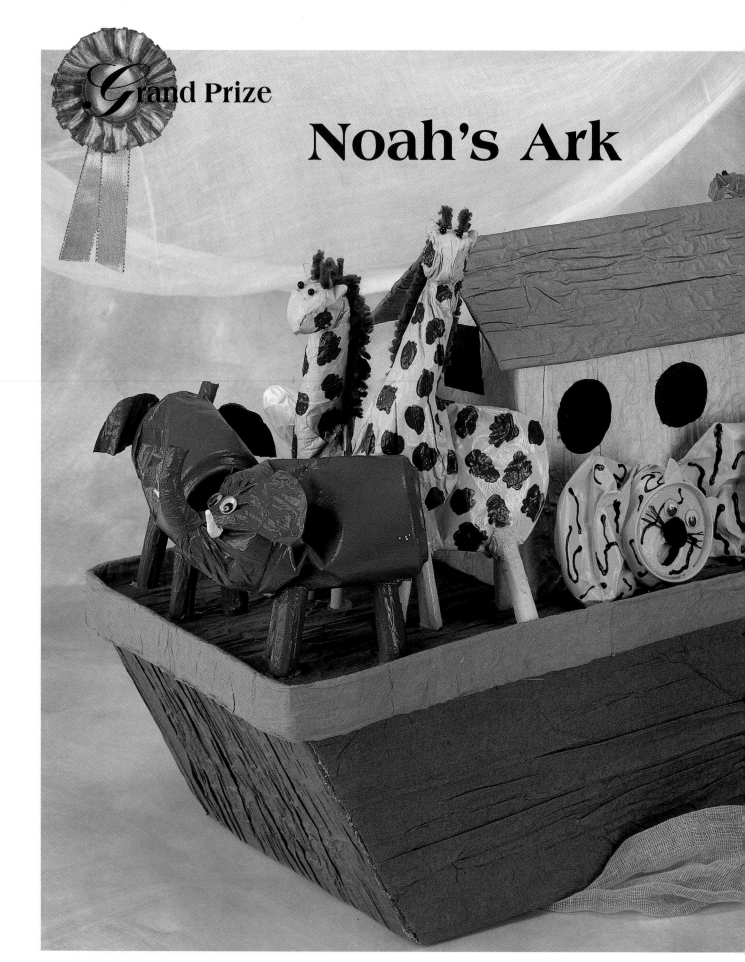

Crafter of the Year

Georgia Skolil
San Pedro, California

"I came up with this idea when planning my niece's baby shower. Her nursery theme was Noah's ark," says Georgia Skolil, our grand-prize winner. "I wanted to carry the theme over to the party. For the table centerpiece I made an ark, complete with crushed-can passengers, and tied balloons to it. For party favors I made individual ark animals from small juice cans and glued a magnet on the back of each so that they could be placed on the refrigerator. I wrote my niece's name and the date of the shower on the back of each crushed-can magnet for a remembrance of the party."

Materials for ark

Paper twist: dark green, cream, black, red, light
   green
3" square cardboard squeegee
Aleene's Designer Tacky Glue™
Cardboard: 1 (10" x 26") piece for deck, 2 (8" x
   26") pieces for body sides, 2 (7" x 10") pieces
   for body front and back, 1 (10" x 20") piece for
   bottom, 2 (5" x 8") pieces for building ends, 2
   (6" x 11") pieces for building sides, 1 (8½" x
   12½") piece for roof, 2 (1½" x 10") strips for
   bow and stern railings, 2 (1½" x 26") strips for
   side railings
Craft knife
Hot-glue gun and glue sticks (optional)

Directions for ark

Note: If paper twist is not large enough to
accommodate cutting dimensions, glue several
strips together to obtain necessary width and
length. When gluing ark pieces, it may be helpful
to use hot-glue gun and glue sticks to hold pieces
together immediately; then use Tacky Glue to
bond pieces permanently.

1 From paper twist, cut the following pieces: 1
(12" x 28") piece, 2 (10" x 28") pieces, 2 (9" x
12") pieces, and 1 (12" x 22") piece from dark
green; 1 (8" x 34") piece from cream; 6
(2"-diameter) circles and 1 (2½") square from
black; 1 (10½" x 14½") piece from red; and 1
(3½" x 74") strip from light green.

2 For deck, using squeegee, spread glue on 1
side of 10" x 26" cardboard piece. Center
deck, glue side down, on 12" x 28" piece of dark
green paper twist. Rub paper twist to secure. Fold
excess paper twist to back and glue. Let dry.

3 Refer to **Diagram A** to complete body sides.
On each 8" x 26" cardboard piece, measure

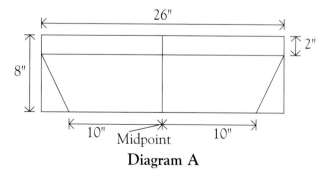

Diagram A

and mark 2" down from 1 long edge on each 8" edge. Draw line to connect marks. Using craft knife, score marked line but do not cut through cardboard. (Scored area will be folded down for platform for ark's deck.) Measure and mark midpoint on opposite long edge of cardboard piece. Then measure and mark 10" on each side of midpoint. Draw lines to connect 10" marks with adjacent 2" marks. Cut along marked diagonal lines. Refer to Step 2 to glue 1 cardboard piece to each 10" x 28" piece of dark green paper twist.

4 Referring to Step 2, for body front and back, glue 7" x 10" cardboard pieces to 9" x 12" pieces of dark green paper twist. For bottom, glue 10" x 20" cardboard piece to 12" x 22" piece of dark green paper twist.

5 Refer to **Diagram B** to complete building ends. On each 5" x 8" cardboard piece, measure and mark midpoint on 1 (5") edge. Then measure and mark 6" up from opposite short edge on each 8" edge. Draw lines to connect 6" marks with midpoint. Cut along marked diagonal lines. On 1 (5" x 8") cardboard piece, measure and mark 2" down from midpoint. Measure and mark 1 (2½") square for window at 2" mark. Cut out.

6 To assemble building, apply glue to 6" ends of each 6" x 11" building side piece. Referring to **Diagram C,** glue side pieces to end pieces along 6" edges. Using squeegee, apply glue to outside of building. Cover building with cream paper twist, slitting paper as needed to fold excess to inside.

Using craft knife, cut an X in paper covering window. Fold resulting paper triangles to inside of building and glue. Evenly space and glue 3 black paper twist circles to each side of building, 1" from top edge. Glue black paper twist square to end of building without window, 2" from top point. Let dry.

7 For roof, using 8½" x 12½" cardboard piece, measure and mark midpoint on each 8½" edge. Draw line to connect midpoints. Using craft knife, score marked line but do not cut through cardboard. Referring to Step 2, glue cardboard roof to 10½" x 14½" piece of red paper twist. Set roof aside.

8 For railing, using squeegee, apply glue to 1 side of each 1½" x 10" cardboard bow and stern railing strip and each 1½" x 26" side railing strip. Referring to **Diagram D** and alternating 10" and 26" lengths, center strips, glue side down, on 3½" x 74" strip of light green paper twist, butting 1½" edges. Fold excess paper twist to back, overlapping edges, and glue. Let dry.

9 To assemble ark, apply glue to 20" ends of 10" x 20" bottom piece. Referring to **Diagram E,** with wrong side of bottom piece faceup, glue 20" edge of body side pieces (wrong sides to inside) to 20" ends of bottom piece. Apply glue to each 7" edge and 1 (10") edge of 7" x 10" body

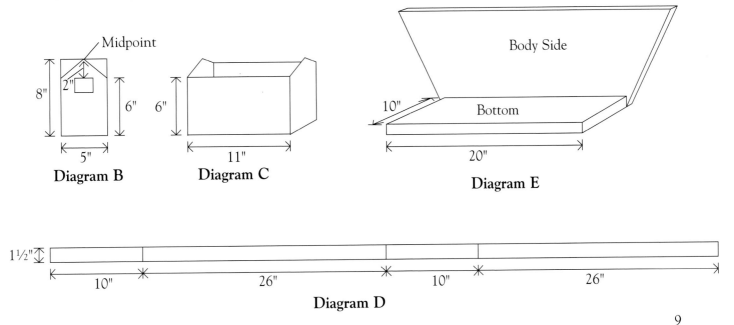

Diagram B

Diagram C

Diagram E

Diagram D

front and back pieces. Glue body front piece to 1 end of ark (wrong side to inside), aligning 7" edges with body side pieces and glue-covered 10" edge with bottom piece. Repeat to glue body back piece to opposite end of ark. Bend scored area of each body side piece to inside to create platform for deck. Apply glue to platform. Glue deck faceup on top of platform. Center and glue building on deck. Do *not* glue roof to building yet. (Roof will be attached later, once camel has been placed inside.) Glue railing to top edge of ark, aligning 1 side railing area with each side of ark and aligning bow and stern areas of railing with front and back of ark. Overlap ends of railing and glue. Let dry.

Materials

For Mr. and Mrs. Noah and each animal: 1 clean, dry aluminum soda can with tab removed (unless otherwise noted)
White primer spray paint
Paintbrushes
Aleene's Right-On Finish™
Aleene's Designer Tacky Glue™
Hot-glue gun and glue sticks
For Mr. and Mrs. Noah: Aleene's Premium-Coat™ Acrylic Paints: Blush, True Red, Dusty Beige, Light Blue
Paper towel
Mop strands: 10 (4") lengths, 1 (8") length
2 (12½") squares fabric for scarves
4 wiggle eyes
For 2 cows: 2 (6" x 12") pieces white posterboard
White paper twist scraps
Aleene's Premium-Coat™ Acrylic Paints: White, Black, Light Fuchsia
Fun Foam scraps: pink, white
4 (4-mm) black beads
4 wiggle eyes
For 2 camels: White paper twist: 1 (12" x 20") piece, 1 (8½" x 12") piece, 1"-wide strips, scraps
Aleene's Premium-Coat™ Acrylic Paint: Dusty Beige
4 (4-mm) black beads
6" x 12" piece white posterboard
For 2 lions: Aleene's Premium-Coat™ Acrylic Paint: Yellow Ochre
Heavy black thread for whiskers
Fun Foam scraps: brown, yellow
4 wiggle eyes
Manila folder
Yarn: gold, brown

Gold thread
For 2 rabbits: Aleene's Premium-Coat™ Acrylic Paints: White, Light Fuchsia
4 (2" x 3") pieces white paper twist
Pom-poms: 4 (¾"-diameter) white, 2 (½"-diameter) pink
4 wiggle eyes
For 2 elephants: White paper twist: 2 (8½" x 12") pieces, 4 (5") squares, 1"-wide strips, scraps
2 (6" x 12") pieces white posterboard
Aleene's Premium-Coat™ Acrylic Paint: Soft Grey
4 wiggle eyes
For 2 giraffes: White paper twist: 2 (14" x 20") pieces, scraps
Yellow Fun Foam scrap
2 (6" x 12") pieces white posterboard
Aleene's Premium-Coat™ Acrylic Paints: Yellow Ochre, Burnt Umber
1 brown chenille stem
4 (4-mm) black beads
Manila folder
Brown yarn
Brown thread
For 2 tigers: Aleene's Premium-Coat™ Acrylic Paints: True Orange, Black
Heavy black thread for whiskers
Fun Foam scraps: black, orange
4 wiggle eyes
Note: General guidelines are given for squashing cans. Cans do not have to be squashed exactly as in models for successful results.

Directions for Mr. and Mrs. Noah

1 To make Mr. Noah, referring to photo, gently bend down section of can rim closest to opening. (Top of can becomes face; chin should rest against body.) Spray can with primer. Let dry. Repeat for Mrs. Noah.

2 Paint face of each can Blush. Let dry. Dilute True Red paint with water. Lightly dab red paint onto cans for cheeks (**Diagram F**). Blot red paint with paper towel. Paint body of Mr. Noah Dusty Beige. Paint body of Mrs. Noah Light Blue. Let dry. Seal cans with Right-On Finish. Let dry.

3 For Mr. Noah, fold 9 (4") mop strands in half. Referring to **Diagram F,** glue strands to face along beard placement line. Let dry. Untwist mop strands. Tie knot in center of remaining 4" mop strand. Glue strand above can opening for mustache. Glue 8" mop strand along top rim of can for hairline.

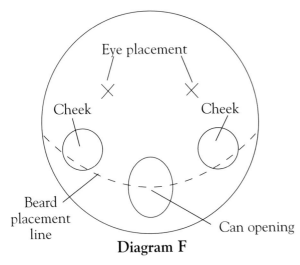

Eye placement

Cheek   Cheek

Beard placement line

Can opening

Diagram F

4 For each scarf, fold 1 fabric square in half diagonally, with wrong sides together. Finger-press fold. Apply glue to back of head area. Referring to photo, center folded edge of fabric over head area. Let dry. Tie ends of fabric into knot under chin. Trim scarves and Mr. Noah's hair and beard to get desired effect. Glue wiggle eyes in place. Let dry.

Directions for animals
Cows

1 Referring to photo, gently dent each can just below top. Spray cans with primer. Let dry.

2 For legs, roll each 6" x 12" piece of posterboard into tube ½" in diameter and 12" in length. Glue to retain shape. Apply glue to entire surface of posterboard tubes. Cover tubes with white paper twist. Let dry. Cut each tube into 4 (3") lengths.

3 Turn each can on its side. Top of each can is cow's face. Paint cans White. Let dry. Randomly paint Black spots on each can. Let dry. Seal with Right-On Finish. Let dry. Referring to photo, glue 4 legs in place on each cow. Let dry.

4 Transfer patterns to Fun Foam and cut 2 muzzles from pink and 4 ears from white. Paint center of each ear Light Fuchsia. Let dry. Spacing beads evenly, glue 2 black beads to center of each muzzle. Referring to photo, glue muzzle, wiggle eyes, and ears in place on each cow. For cow with horns, roll each of 2 small scraps of white paper twist into cone shape. Glue horns to 1 cow between ears. Let dry.

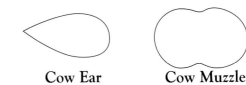

Cow Ear   **Cow Muzzle**

Camels

Note: Camel poking head out of ark window does not require soda can.

1 For camel in window, roll and twist 12" x 20" piece of paper twist into tube. Bend 1 end of tube under several times to form head. Glue folded head to retain shape. Let dry. Slightly spread out unfolded end of paper twist to form lower part of neck and chest. Stuff tube slightly with small pieces of paper twist to fill out neck. For each ear, roll small scrap of paper twist into cone shape. Referring to photo for spacing, glue ears in place on top of head. Let dry.

2 Wrap and glue strips of paper twist around neck and head. Let dry. Paint head Dusty Beige. Let dry. Seal with Right-On Finish. Let dry. For eyes, glue 2 black beads on head in front of ears. Referring to photo, insert neck of camel through window in building and glue in place on wrong side of building. Let dry.

3 Bend roof of building along scored line. Apply glue to top edges of building. Glue roof to building. Let dry.

4 For remaining camel, referring to photo, gently dent center of can. Spray can with primer. Let dry.

5 Fold under 1" along 1 (8½") edge of 8½" x 12" piece of paper twist. Referring to **Diagram G,** glue folded edge of paper twist to top rim of can, overlapping ends. Drop scraps of paper twist into resulting tube. (Top of can becomes chest, and paper scraps pad chest area.) Turn can on its side. Twist tube tightly. Bend twisted tube up to create neck. Fold end under several times as in Step 1 for Camels to create head. Glue folded head to retain shape. Let dry. Make and attach ears as in Step 1 for Camels.

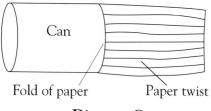

Diagram G

6 For humps, form paper twist scraps into 2 (1"-diameter) balls. Referring to photo and spacing evenly, glue humps on body of camel. Wrap and glue strips of paper twist around neck, head, and body. Let dry.

7 To make legs, refer to Step 2 for Cows. Referring to photo, glue legs in place on camel. Paint entire camel Dusty Beige. Let dry. Seal with Right-On Finish. Let dry. For eyes, glue 2 black beads on head in front of ears. Let dry.

Lions

1 Referring to photo, squash each can at an angle. (Top of each can becomes lion's face.) Spray cans with primer. Let dry.

Paint cans Yellow Ochre. Let dry. Seal with Right-On Finish. Let dry.

2 For whiskers, cut 10 (2½") lengths of heavy black thread. Group 5 threads and tie knot in

Lion and Tiger Ear   **Lion and Tiger Nose**

center. Repeat with remaining 5 threads. Glue 1 group of threads to top of each can, just above opening. Let dry.

3 Transfer patterns to Fun Foam and cut 2 noses from brown and 2 ears from yellow. Referring to photo, glue noses in place on top of black threads. Trim threads to get desired effect. Glue 2 wiggle eyes in place on each face. For 1 lion, glue ears in place along top rim of can. Let dry.

4 Cut 2" x 8½" rectangle from manila folder. Holding gold and brown yarn as 1, wrap yarn widthwise around length of rectangle. Machine-stitch lengthwise along center of rectangle. Clip looped ends of yarn and tear yarn away from rectangle.

5 For lion without ears, glue stitched yarn around outside of rim for mane. Let dry. Trim yarn to get desired effect. For tail, using 1 (4") length of brown yarn and 2 (4") lengths of gold yarn, braid yarn lengths together, knotting ends. Glue tail in place on bottom of can. Let dry.

Rabbits

1 Referring to photo, squash each can so that bottom of can is directly behind top of can. Spray cans with primer. Let dry. Paint cans White. Let dry.

2 For ears, fold each piece of paper twist in half to measure 1" x 3". Twist each end of each piece tightly. Fan out center section of each piece of paper twist, while shaping to curve inward. Fold twisted ends to inside of each ear and glue in place. Let dry. Paint inside of each ear Light Fuchsia. Let dry. Referring to photo, glue 2 ears in place on each can. Let dry.

3 Seal all painted areas with Right-On Finish. Let dry. Referring to photo, glue 2 white pom-poms in place on each can, just above opening. Then glue 1 pink pom-pom on each can, just above white pom-poms. Glue 2 wiggle eyes in place on each can. Let dry.

Elephants

1 Referring to photo, gently dent cans just below top. Spray cans with primer. Let dry.

2 To make each elephant trunk, referring to Step 5 for Camels, glue 1 folded 8½" x 12" piece of paper twist to top rim of 1 can. Lightly stuff base of tube with scraps of paper twist. Twist tube tightly. Turn can on its side. Referring to photo, curve twisted tube up. Trim trunk for desired effect. Glue strips of paper twist around trunk to hold shape. Let dry.

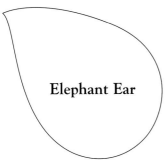

Elephant Ear

3 For each pair of ears, glue 2 (5") square pieces of paper twist together. Let dry. Transfer pattern to glued paper twist and cut 2 ears. Referring to photo, glue 2 ears in place on each elephant's head. Let dry.

4 To make legs, refer to Step 2 for Cows. Glue 4 legs in place on each elephant. Let dry. Paint elephants Soft Grey. Let dry. Seal with Right-On Finish. Let dry.

5 To make tusks, cut 4 (1½") scraps of white paper twist and roll each into tube. Curve each tube upward. Referring to photo, glue 2 tusks in place on each elephant. Glue 2 wiggle eyes in place on each elephant. Let dry.

Giraffes

1 Referring to photo, squash each can at an angle.

2 Referring to Step 5 for Camels and using 14" x 20" pieces of paper twist, make and attach 1 giraffe neck and head to each can.

3 Transfer ear pattern to yellow Fun Foam and cut 4. Referring to photo, glue 2 ears in place on each giraffe head. To make legs, refer to Step 2 for Cows. Referring to photo, glue 4 legs in place on each giraffe. Let dry.

Giraffe Ear

4 Paint giraffes Yellow Ochre. Let dry. Randomly paint Burnt Umber spots on each can. Let dry. Seal with Right-On Finish. Let dry.

5 For horns, cut 4 (¾") lengths from chenille stem. Referring to photo, glue 2 horns in place on each giraffe. Glue 2 black beads in place on each giraffe for eyes. Let dry.

6 Referring to Step 5 for Lions and using 1" x 4" piece of manila folder and brown yarn, make 1 mane for each giraffe. Glue 1 mane in place on each giraffe along back of neck. Let dry.

Tigers

1 Referring to photo, squash each can at an angle. (Top of each can becomes tiger's face.) Spray cans with primer. Let dry.

2 Paint cans True Orange. Let dry. Randomly paint Black stripes on each can. Let dry. Seal with Right-On Finish. Let dry.

3 Referring to Step 2 for Lions, make and attach whiskers to each tiger. Transfer patterns (see Lions) to Fun Foam and cut 2 noses from black and 4 ears from orange. Referring to Step 3 for Lions, attach noses, ears, and wiggle eyes to tigers. Let dry.

*M*ost Creative Use of an Aleene's Product

Lynda Ostrom Nord
Saint Peter, Minnesota

*"My husband, Ron, found this
old tray at a garage sale," says Lynda
Ostrom Nord. "He told me that when he
saw it he figured I could make something
out of it, so he bought it for two dollars.
After I completed the mosaic tray,
it was Ron who convinced me to
enter it in the contest."*

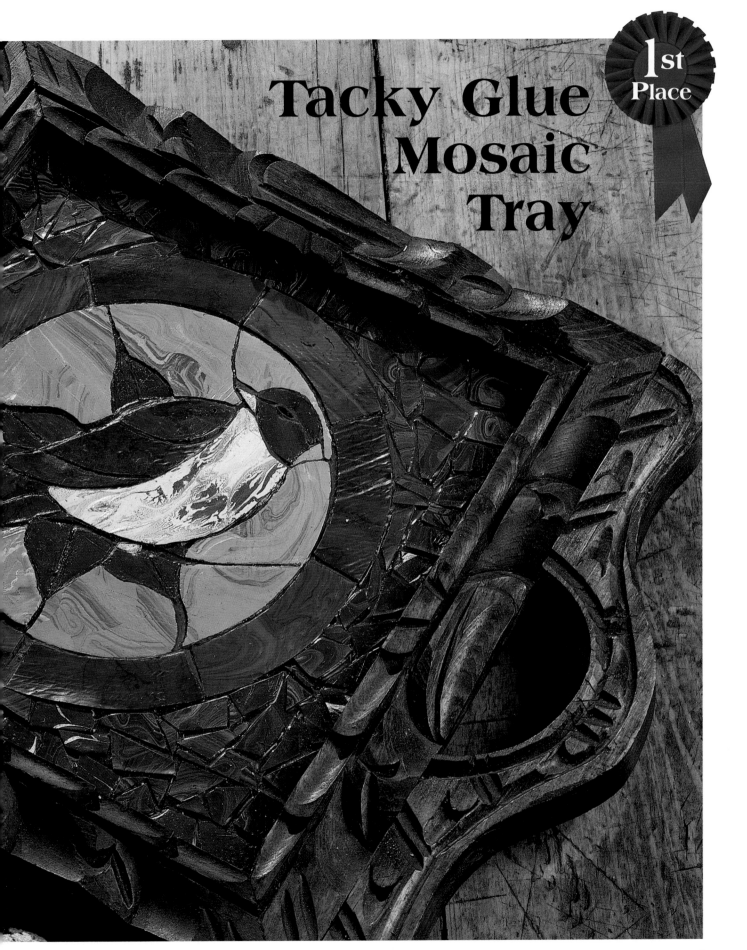

Tacky Glue Mosaic Tray

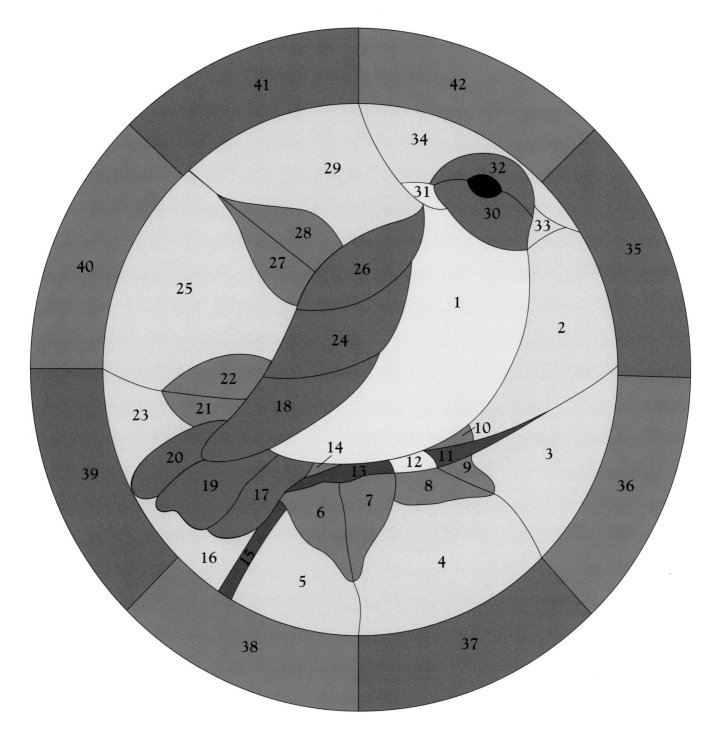

Materials

Wooden tray with clear glass bottom*
Aleene's Premium-Coat™ Acrylic Paints: Deep
    Green, Black, Gold, Ivory, Deep Mauve, Light
    Fuchsia, Burnt Umber, Light Blue, Medium
    Blue, White
Aleene's Tacky Glue™
9 paper cups
Wooden craft sticks
Transparent tape
Plastic wrap
2 sheets tracing paper
Straight pin or ballpoint pen
Scissors: regular, embroidery for cutting small
    pieces of faux tile
Cold cream
Plastic squeeze bottle with nozzle tip
Tweezers to position tiles (optional)
Toothpick
Small paintbrush
    *Note: If you prefer, use picture frame. Attach
drawer handles to sides of frame to convert it into
tray.

Directions

1 Mix ¼ cup of Deep Green paint and ¼ cup
of Tacky Glue in paper cup. Stir thoroughly,
using wooden craft stick. To create marbleized
effect, add a few drops each of Black and Gold to
Deep Green base mixture. Stir once or twice to
swirl colors. Using separate paper cups for each,
repeat to mix glue with following paints: Deep
Green for base and drops of Black and Ivory; Deep
Mauve for base and drops of Black; Light Fuchsia
for base and drops of Deep Mauve and Gold;
Burnt Umber for base; Light Blue for base and
drops of Medium Blue and White; and Deep
Green base. Using equal parts of Gold paint and
Tacky Glue, mix small amount of each for beak
and foot.

2 Tape several large pieces of plastic wrap to a
level, flat surface. Pour each mixture into separate puddle on plastic wrap. Using craft stick,
smooth each mixture to approximately ⅛" thick.
Let mixtures dry *thoroughly* (this may take several

days). Peel dried mixtures from plastic wrap. If any
mixture is at all sticky, stop peeling and let dry for
another day.

3 Transfer complete pattern to each sheet of
tracing paper. Leave 1 pattern intact. Cut
remaining pattern apart, making individual patterns for each numbered piece.

4 Referring to photo and pattern for colors,
tape each piece to corresponding mixture.
(Leaves are cut from solid Deep Green mixture,
tiles encircling bird are cut from Deep Green mixture with Black and Ivory swirls, and eye will be
made later by applying Black paint straight from
bottle.) Using straight pin, poke holes along edges
of each pattern piece; if you prefer, use ballpoint
pen to trace each piece. Using regular scissors for
large pieces and embroidery scissors for small
pieces, cut out tiles just inside marked lines. Trim
any ragged edges. For tiles framing pattern, cut
abstract shapes from Deep Green mixture with
Black and Gold swirls. Leave small amount of
mixture uncut so that you can custom-cut filler
pieces later. Apply thin layer of cold cream to top
of each tile. (Cold cream will prevent grout from
adhering to tops.) Center uncut pattern faceup
under glass from tray. Tape in place.

5 To make grout, thoroughly mix equal parts of
Black paint and Tacky Glue. Fill squeeze bottle with grout mixture. Working on small section
at a time and laying tiles in numerical order, apply
grout to glass with squeeze bottle. Smooth grout to
⅛" thickness, using craft stick. Position tiles 1 at a
time and tap into place to complete design (it
may be helpful to use tweezers). Fill in remainder
of area around pattern in same manner, using
abstract-shaped tiles. Custom-cut filler pieces as
necessary. When all tiles are in place, add more
grout where needed. (Carefully remove any excess
grout before it begins to set, using toothpick.)
Using Black paint straight from bottle and small
paintbrush, fill in eye. Let tray dry
thoroughly. If desired, have piece of glass cut to fit
over mosaic to protect from spills.

Fishing Bobber Santa Pin

by Debra Rounell Robertson
LaPorte, Texas

"When I was cleaning out my husband's fishing box, I found a fishing bobber. I looked at it, turning it around and around, trying to decide what it resembled," says Debra Robertson. "I finally decided I could turn it into a Santa pin. It was such a simple and fun project."

Materials
1 medium-sized red-and-white fishing bobber
Aleene's Designer Tacky Glue™
Pom-poms: 1 (½"-diameter) white with sparkles,
   1 (¼"-diameter) red
White curly hair
2 wiggle eyes
1 small pin back

Directions
With bobber red side up, glue white pom-pom to top. Let dry. Referring to photo, glue curly hair around bottom of bobber for beard. Let dry. Glue wiggle eyes and red pom-pom nose in place. Let dry. Glue pin back to back of bobber. Let dry.

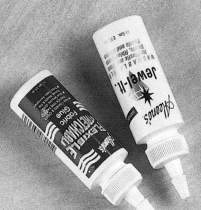

To order
Aleene's products, call
Aleene's consumer services at
1-800-825-3363.

Wonderful Wearables

**Jeanie Sexton
Kuttawa, Kentucky**

"My minister asked me to design a banner to represent our church at the Procession of Banners for the 1996 annual conference," says Jeanie Sexton. *"I knew the effect I wanted, but I had not yet developed the technique. I created the vest as a sample to experiment with the faux stained-glass effect. The secret is to allow the steam and the heat from the iron to pucker the lamé. The combination of steam and heat shrinks the fabric and creates little bubbles, resulting in a stained-glass look!"*

Materials

Purchased vest pattern
Lining fabric (See pattern for yardage.)
Tissue lamé: bronze (See pattern for yardage.),
    12" squares in variety of bright colors
Low-loft batting (same yardage as for vest)
Organdy: 12" square for each motif, same yardage
    as for vest
Aleene's Shrink-It™ Plastic
Aleene's Fusible Web™
Aleene's Stop Fraying Glue™
Aleene's Baking Board
Clear .004 monofilament thread
Flexible braid: ⅛"-wide black flat for leading,
    narrow metallic for antennae
Aleene's Flexible Stretchable™ Fabric Glue
Crewel hand needle
Machine embroidery thread: black 40-weight
    rayon, bronze metallic for background quilting
#80/12 machine needle
Twin needle (optional)
Open-toe machine appliqué foot
Aleene's Stick Glue™

Directions

Note: Patterns provided are full size for appliqués that appear on vest front. Appliqués that appear on back are made from enlarged patterns. Enlarge or reduce patterns on a copier as desired for larger or smaller motifs. If you enlarge patterns, you'll need larger squares of tissue lamé and organdy. Each should be at least 2" larger along all edges than appliqué pattern pieces.

1 Using purchased pattern, cut out vest from lining fabric. Adding 2" along all edges of vest pieces, cut out vest from bronze lamé, batting, and organdy. (Added 2" allows for shrinkage when quilting.) Set all vest pieces aside.

2 To make appliqués, place piece of Shrink-It on ironing board. Lay 1 (12") square of tissue lamé on top. With iron set on steam and hottest setting, hold iron as close as possible to fabric *without* actually touching fabric. (If your iron has feature that emits burst of steam, use it.) Fabric will bubble and shrink. Once fabric has stopped

Faux Stained-Glass Vest

bubbling, let it cool; then repeat process to shrink fabric a bit more. Repeat with remaining squares of lamé.

3 Trace appliqué patterns onto paper side of fusible web, making individual patterns for each section. Cut out pieces slightly larger than traced. Place 1 fusible web pattern piece, paper side down, on piece of Shrink-It. Place desired steamed lamé square on top. Steam lamé with iron in same manner as before. (Fusible web will adhere to lamé without touching pieces with iron.) Repeat with remaining pattern pieces and steamed lamé squares. Cut out appliqué pieces along marked lines. Peel off paper backing of fusible web. Lightly coat edges of appliqué pieces with Stop Fraying Glue.

4 For each motif to be applied to vest, center and trace entire motif onto square of organdy, adding leaves as desired to flower. Place baking board on ironing board. Set iron on nylon/silk setting. Position appliqué pieces, 1 at a time, onto corresponding areas outlined on organdy. (Slip leaves under outside edges of flower as desired. All other edges of appliqués will be butted rather than overlapped, as with traditional appliqué.) Steam appliqué pieces to organdy in same manner as before. If pieces do not adhere well, lightly touch fabric edges with iron, being careful not to iron out bubbles. Do *not* iron back and forth. Using clear monofilament thread and medium stitch length, stitch around each piece, close to the edges.

5 For imitation leading lines that outline appliqué pieces, cut lengths of ⅛"-wide black braid to correspond to individual numbered areas, adding 4" to each length. Apply thin line of Flexible Stretchable Fabric Glue along edge of 1 leaf. Leaving 2" tail at each end, gently press 1 length of braid leading into glue line. Let dry. Thread 1 end of braid leading length onto crewel needle and pull to back. Repeat with remaining braid end. Continue in same manner to place leading around remaining appliqué pieces, following numerical order marked on appliqué patterns. Let dry. Using black rayon thread, straightstitch

down center of all braid leading. Alternatively, stitch braid leading using twin needle, catching both edges of braid.

6 Trim excess organdy from edges of appliqués. Lightly coat outer edges of appliqués with Stop Fraying Glue. Determine position for appliqués on bronze lamé vest pieces. Apply stick glue to wrong side of appliqués along edges and glue in place. (If you wish to add leading to vest background areas as shown in photo, tuck ends of black braid under appliqués *before* gluing appliqués in place. Allow leading to flow in curves to edges of vest pieces. Stitch leading as before. For leaded motif without stained glass, transfer motif to vest piece and stitch leading as before.)

7 For butterfly antennae, using Flexible Stretchable Fabric Glue and referring to photos, glue narrow metallic braid lengths in place, leaving 1" free at each cut end. Let dry. Thread 1 end of 1 braid leading length onto

61

crewel needle and pull to back. Repeat with remaining braid ends. Using clear monofilament thread and narrow zigzag stitch, couch over braid.

8 To stitch appliqués in place, using black rayon thread, straightstitch down center of all braid leading. Alternatively, stitch braid leading using twin needle, catching both edges of braid.

9 Stack organdy, batting, and appliquéd vest pieces right side up. If desired, trace motifs onto lamé vest piece for quilting pattern. Using bronze metallic thread, machine-quilt each traced motif. Stipple-quilt background of each vest piece. Recut vest according to vest pattern. (Vest was cut 2" larger in Step 1 to allow for shrinkage when quilting.) To complete vest, referring to directions included with vest pattern.

Miniblind Earrings

by Joann Barsich
Hammond, Indiana

"After installing new vinyl miniblinds in my living room, I had lots of extra slats left over," says Joann Barsich. "I didn't want to throw them out, so I played around with them and came up with these earrings!"

Materials

For each: Vinyl miniblind slat
Fine-grade sandpaper
Ice pick
Clear acrylic spray sealer
Pliers
1 pair fishhook earrings
For chili peppers: Aleene's Premium-Coat™ Acrylic Paints: True Red, True Green
Small paintbrush
2 jump rings
For polka dots: dimensional craft paints with tip: orange, bright pink, light green
6 jump rings

Directions for chili pepper earrings

1 Cut 2 (3") lengths from vinyl slat. Sand both sides. Transfer pattern to 1 length. Reverse pattern and transfer to remaining length. Cut out.

2 Paint 1 side of each chili pepper bottom True Red. Let dry. Then paint top of each chili pepper True Green. Let dry. Repeat to paint remaining side of each chili pepper. Using ice pick, poke hole in stem of each chili pepper.

3 Coat 1 side of each chili pepper with spray sealer. Let dry. Spray remaining side of each chili pepper. Using pliers and 1 jump ring, attach 1 chili pepper to each fishhook earring.

Directions for polka-dot earrings

1 Cut 6 (½" x 1⅛") rectangles from miniblind slat. Sand 1 side of each rectangle. Referring to photo and using orange paint, paint 3 rows of polka dots on sanded side of 2 rectangles. Repeat with remaining rectangles, using bright pink paint for 2 rectangles and light green paint for remaining rectangles. Let dry.

2 Using ice pick, center and poke 1 hole along 1 long edge of each orange-dotted rectangle. Poke 2 holes along opposite long edge of each, with holes equidistant from short edge. Center and poke 1 hole along 1 short edge of each pink-dotted rectangle and each green-dotted rectangle. Coat painted side of each rectangle with spray sealer. Let dry.

3 Using pliers and 1 jump ring, attach 1 orange-dotted rectangle to each fishhook earring. Using 1 jump ring each, attach 1 pink-dotted rectangle and 1 green-dotted rectangle to lower edge of each orange-dotted rectangle.

Thread Dough Necklace

by Jackie Patton
Plainville, Massachusetts

"I just can't stand seeing anything go to waste—not even the tangled mess of threads that appears in my thread drawer after many rummages through it," Jackie Patton says. "The jumble of color often ends up in many handmade paper projects and was the inspiration behind these beads."

Materials

Waxed paper
Cornstarch
Aleene's Tacky Glue™
Butter knife
Zip-top plastic bag
Thread: scraps of assorted colors, variegated
   metallic
Rotary cutter and mat
Aleene's Premium-Coat™ Acrylic Paints: Dusty
   Blue, Soft Fuchsia
Toothpick
Razor blade
26" (20-pound test) fishing line
Blue iridescent seed beads
Barrel clasp

Directions

1 Cover work surface with sheet of waxed paper. Sprinkle 3 tablespoons of cornstarch in center of waxed paper. Squeeze layer of Tacky Glue on top of cornstarch. Using butter knife, fold glue into cornstarch, adding more glue as necessary until mixture holds together. Knead mixture until smooth, pliable, and claylike in consistency, adding cornstarch if necessary to keep from becoming sticky. When not working with dough, store in zip-top bag. (Dough can be stored for 3 to 4 days.)

2 Wind thread scraps 12 to 15 times around 3 or 4 fingers. Slide threads off fingers. Place threads on mat and cut across threads every ¼" along entire length, using rotary cutter. Cut some thread segments again to make different lengths.

3 Divide dough in half. Flatten 1 half in your hand, making small well in center. Pour small amount of Dusty Blue paint into well. Add some cut-up threads. Knead dough until paint and threads are thoroughly incorporated. Continue adding paint and threads, a little at a time, until desired affect is achieved. Store in zip-top bag. Repeat with remaining half of dough, using Soft Fuchsia paint.

4 Wrap variegated metallic thread tightly around dough, burying thread into dough with toothpick. Roll dough in hands to shape into ball. To make beads, roll small amount of dough between palms to shape into varying sizes of round beads. If desired, roll small amounts of Soft Fuchsia and Dusty Blue dough together to form two-tone beads. To make square beads, shape dough into rectangular log about ½" thick. Using razor blade, cut log to form cubes. To make holes in beads, gently insert toothpick through center of each bead. Let beads dry. If threads pop out on any bead when dough is dry, put dot of glue in your palm and roll bead between palms until threads stick down. Let dry.

5 Referring to photo, thread dough beads onto fishing line length, placing 1 seed bead between each dough bead and completing each end with series of seed beads. Attach barrel clasp to ends of fishing line.

Snowman Family Sweatshirts

by Kathleen Fitzgerald Wood
Slippery Rock, Pennsylvania

"In this mountainous region, we have our fair share of snowfall and winter fun," says Kathleen Wood. *"One day I asked my husband, son, and daughter, 'If you were a snowman, what would you look like?' Together we dug through fabric scraps and craft supplies. We made a few sketches, and then our personal snowman family came to life!"*

Materials (for 1 sweatshirt)

Sweatshirt in desired color
Fabrics: 10" square white, 2" x 6" piece orange, scraps in variety of colors and prints
Aleene's Fusible Web™
Powdered blush
Dimensional fabric paints with tip: black, iridescent glitter, orange, green (optional), red (optional)
⅜"-wide ribbon (optional)
Aleene's Jewel-It™ Glue (optional)

Directions

1 Wash and dry sweatshirt; do not use fabric softener in washer or dryer.

2 From white fabric, cut 1 (8¼"-diameter) circle for adult snowman head or 1 (6⅝"-diameter) circle for child snowman head. Transfer 1 nose pattern in desired size to orange fabric and cut out. Referring to photo for inspiration, cut out personalized snowman accessories (top hat, bow tie, bonnet, hat, scarf, earmuffs) from fabric scraps.

3 Fuse web to wrong side of each fabric piece. Trim excess webbing. Remove paper backing. Fuse head to sweatshirt front. Fuse nose and accessories in place.

4 Apply cheeks, using powdered blush. Using black paint, paint eyes and dotted mouth. Let dry. Using iridescent glitter paint, paint icicle hair, eyebrows, and accent in eyes. For father snowman, also use iridescent glitter paint to add mustache and beard if desired. Let dry. Outline snowman head and accessories, using fabric paint. Let dry. For mother snowman, use Jewel-It to glue ribbon in place for bonnet ties if desired. Let dry. Do not wash sweatshirt for at least 2 weeks. Turn sweatshirt wrong side out, wash by hand, and hang to dry.

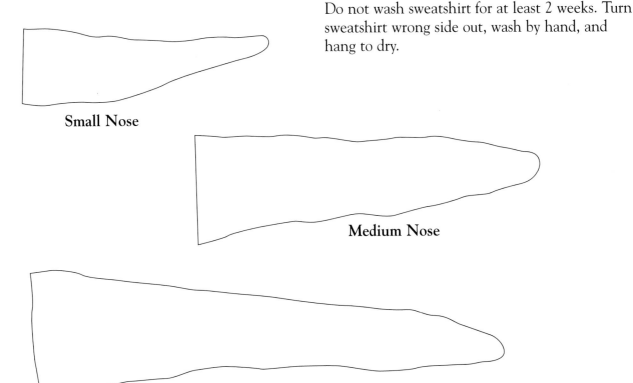

Small Nose

Medium Nose

Large Nose

Smiley T-shirt & Earrings

by Karen Gargac Sánchez
Weslaco, Texas

"My husband, Raul, can't always accompany me when I visit my family in Toledo, so sometimes I end up flying alone with our three little girls," says Karen Gargac Sánchez. "We often have to go through as many as three different airports. I decided to dress us alike to help keep track of the girls. It also makes it less likely that someone would try to grab one part of a matching set. Besides, the girls look so adorable, no one seems to get too upset if they get a bit restless on the plane!"

Materials (for 1 T-shirt)
White T-shirt
Cardboard covered with waxed paper
Pop-up craft sponges
Aleene's Premium-Coat™ Acrylic Paints: variety of colors, Black
Aleene's Enhancers™ Textile Medium
Styrofoam meat trays
Paper towels
Paintbrush

Materials (for 1 pair of earrings)
Aleene's Opake Shrink-It™ Plastic
Fine-grade sandpaper
Fine-tip permanent black marker
Colored pencils in variety of colors
⅛"-diameter hole punch
Aleene's Baking Board or brown paper bag
Talcum powder (optional)
Aleene's Right-On Finish™ or Aleene's Glaze-It™
Toothpick
Pliers
4 jump rings
1 pair fishhook earrings

Directions

1 **For T-shirt,** wash and dry shirt; do not use fabric softener in washer or dryer. Lay shirt flat on clean work surface. Place cardboard covered with waxed paper inside T-shirt. Cut pop-up sponges in various sizes of circles. Place each sponge circle in water to expand and wring out excess water. For each color of paint, mix equal parts paint and textile medium. Pour small puddles of each mixed paint onto foam trays, using a separate tray for each color of paint.

2 Working with 1 face color at a time, dip 1 sponge circle into paint and blot excess paint on paper towel. Referring to photo and working in sections, press sponge onto front of shirt and sleeves to paint circles. Repeat with remaining sponge circles and paints as desired, rinsing each sponge between colors. Let dry. Repeat to paint back of sleeves only. Let dry.

3 Referring to photo and using Black paint, paint eyes and mouth. Let dry. Do not wash T-shirt for at least 1 week. Turn T-shirt wrong side out, wash by hand, and hang to dry.

4 **For earrings,** sand both sides of sheet of Shrink-It so that markings will adhere. Be sure to thoroughly sand both vertically and horizontally. Using black marker, trace pattern twice onto 1 side of Shrink-It. (Marker ink may run on sanded surface; runs will shrink and disappear

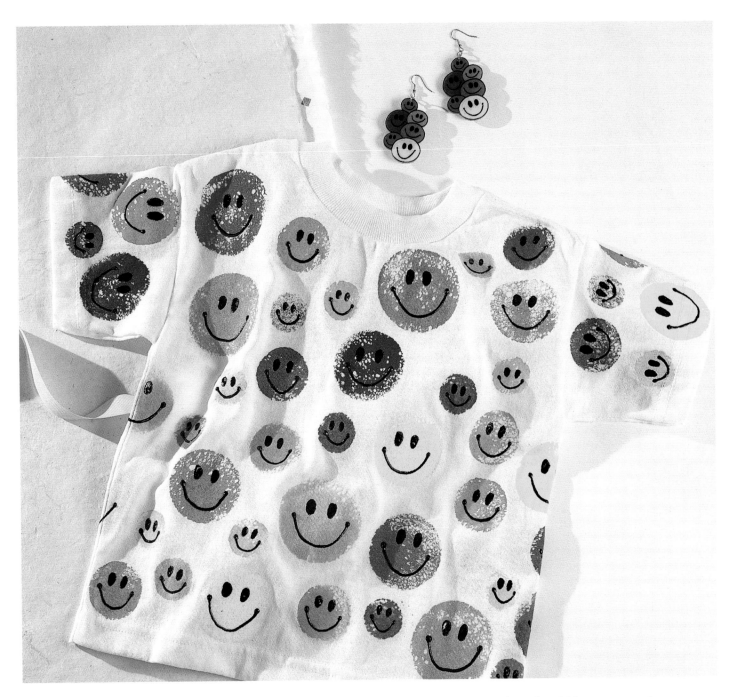

during baking.) Trace drawn lines on opposite side of Shrink-It.

5 Referring to photo, use colored pencils to color both sides of Shrink-It with face colors. Using black marker, draw eyes and mouth on each. Punch holes where indicated.

6 Preheat toaster oven or conventional oven to 275° to 300°. Place each design on room-temperature baking board or on nonprinted side of brown bag that has a little talcum powder sprinkled on it; bake in oven. Edges should begin to curl within 25 seconds; if not, increase temperature slightly. If edges begin to curl as soon as designs are put in oven, reduce temperature. After about 1 minute, designs will lie flat. Remove each design from oven. Let cool. Coat both sides of designs with 2 to 3 coats of Right-On Finish or Glaze-It, letting dry between coats and keeping holes clear with toothpick. Let dry.

7 Using pliers and 2 jump rings, attach 1 design to each fishhook earring.

Honorable Mention

Puzzle Shirt

by Linda Frost
Pocatello, Idaho

"The idea for the puzzle T-shirt came from my mother, who loves jigsaw puzzles," says Linda Frost. "She has spent many hours working puzzles with my children. A puzzle just seemed like a fun idea for a T-shirt."

Materials

White T-shirt
Scenic fabric panel*
Aleene's Fusible Web™
Buttons
Paintbrush
Aleene's OK to Wash-It™ Glue

*Note: If you cannot find a ready-made fabric panel you like, you can make your own. Overlap fabric pieces ¼" and fuse. Add embellishments as desired.

Directions

1 Wash and dry shirt and fabric panel; do not use fabric softener in washer or dryer. Using fabric panel as guide, cut 1 piece of equal size from fusible web. Referring to **Diagram,** on paper side of fusible web, use pencil and ruler to make a grid. Using grid as guide, draw puzzle shapes. Do *not* cut out shapes. Fuse web to wrong side of fabric panel.

2 Cut out puzzle pieces. Referring to photo, place puzzle pieces on shirt front as desired. (You may want to put part of puzzle together and scatter other puzzle pieces across T-shirt.) Fuse puzzle pieces in place. Embellish with buttons as desired. Using paintbrush, brush washable glue around edges of each puzzle piece to prevent fraying. Let dry.

Diagram

Screen Rose Brooch

by Danie Fontenot
Washington, Louisiana

"While scanning the shopping channels on TV, a beautiful and expensive designer brooch caught my eye," says Danie Fontenot. "It was made of gold filigree and was in the shape of a rose. Two things instantly came to mind: Heidi's window screen jewelry and the window screens that maintenance had just changed out in my apartment complex. I retrieved some discarded screens, and three days later I was wearing my beautiful and inexpensive Screen Rose Brooch."

Materials

8½" x 11" piece wire or plastic screen
Gold spray paint
8½" x 11" sheet paper
Transparent tape
8½" x 11" piece cardboard
Plastic wrap
Aleene's 3-D Foiling™ Glue
Gold press-and-peel craft foil
Clear acrylic spray sealer
Antiquing medium
Gold wire thread
Aleene's Tacky Glue™
Bar pin back

Directions

1 Using 2 coats of paint, spray-paint 1 side of screen gold, letting paint dry between coats. Repeat on remaining side of screen.

2 Transfer 5 petal As, 4 petal Bs, 3 petal Cs, and 1 center to sheet of paper. Do not cut out patterns. Tape paper to cardboard, with patterns faceup. Cover with plastic wrap. Tape screen to plastic wrap.

3 Using 3-D Foiling Glue, trace all pattern lines except straight bottom edges. Wait 15 minutes. (Glue will drain into screen.) Repeat process. Let dry 24 hours. (Glue will be opaque and sticky when dry. Glue must be thoroughly dry before foil is applied.)

4 Before removing screen from plastic wrap, lay foil dull side down on top of glue lines. Using fingers or pencil grip, gently but firmly press foil onto glue, completely covering glue with foil. Be sure to press foil into crevices. Peel away foil paper. If any part of glue lines is not covered, reapply foil as needed. Remove screen from plastic wrap. Turn screen over and repeat foiling process. Cut out petals and center, trimming as close as possible to foil. Spray each piece with acrylic spray sealer. Let dry. Referring to manufacturer's instructions, apply antiquing medium to each piece. Let dry. Apply second coat of acrylic spray sealer to each piece. Let dry.

5 To assemble rose, beginning at 1 end, roll up center to form bud (see photo). Crinkle bottom straight edge of bud and wrap with gold wire thread to hold in place. Beginning with 1 petal C, crinkle bottom and then wrap petal around bud, using wire thread to hold in place. Continue in same manner, using remaining petal Cs, petal Bs, and then petal As. Press petals down gently to separate. Apply Tacky Glue between layers of petals at base. Allow glue to dry slightly. Shape petals. Let glue dry thoroughly. Trim bottom of rose as close to wire thread as possible.

6 Cut 1 (1¼"-diameter) circle and 1 (¾" x 1") rectangle from cardboard. Spray-paint 1 side of circle and 1 side of rectangle gold. Let dry. Repeat on remaining sides. Using Tacky Glue, glue rose to 1 side of cardboard circle. Let dry. Glue pin back to remaining side of cardboard circle. Open pin. Glue rectangle over base of pin to secure pin base.

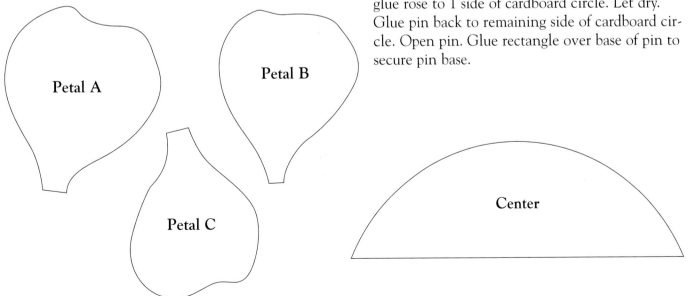

Petal A

Petal B

Petal C

Center

Crafts for Kids

Corn Costume

Susanne Petrucci
De Kalb, Illinois

"We live in the middle of corn country," says Susanne Petrucci. *"Each year the city hosts a Corn Festival. After seeing all the corn-related items at the festival, my oldest son thought it would be fun to dress up as an ear of corn for Halloween. I came up with this costume for him."*

Materials
Yellow adult-sized T-shirt
Cardboard covered with waxed paper
Aleene's Designer Tacky Glue™
4 (100-count) bags yellow cotton balls
Clear acrylic spray sealer
1½ yards green felt
4 (12") lengths florist's wire

Directions
Note: Neck of shirt comes over back of child's head. Child should wear a green turtleneck and green tights or sweatpants under costume.

1 Cut and discard sleeves from T-shirt. Place cardboard covered with waxed paper inside shirt. Beginning at center front, glue 1 row of cotton balls from neckline to bottom of shirt. Repeat to glue 6 more rows on each side of center row. Let dry. Turn shirt over. In same manner, glue rows of cotton balls to back of shirt, starting at neckline and stopping even with bottom of sleeve openings. Let dry. Lightly spray entire shirt with acrylic spray sealer. Let dry.

2 From felt, cut 4 (9" x 40") strips and 6 (8⅛" x 16½") strips, tapering 1 end of each strip to a point. Lay 1 long strip on work surface. Bend 1 length of florist's wire into U shape. Referring to **Diagram A,** place wire at edge of strip, about 5" from point and with curved end of wire toward point of felt. With points even, overlap long strip with 1 short strip and glue in place, covering wire. Repeat to glue another long strip and short strip together. Then make 2 sets of 2 short strips each.

3 Referring to **Diagram B,** with bottom of 1 remaining long felt strip aligned with bottom of shirt, glue 1 long edge to front of shirt, aligning with last row of cotton balls. Cut slit at armhole. Fold remaining edge of strip to back of shirt; align and glue in same manner. Let dry. Repeat to glue remaining long strip to other side of shirt.

Glue straight bottom edges of short strip sets across back of shirt below bottom edge of cotton balls, overlapping strips as you work. Let dry. Glue longer strip sets to back of shirt, aligning straight bottom of strips with bottom of shirt, making sure to glue up to bottom edge of cotton balls. Let dry.

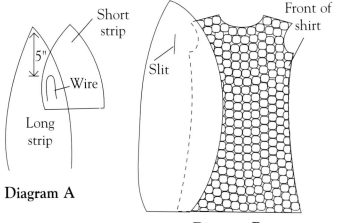

Diagram A

Diagram B

Walnut Birds

Honorable Mention

by Tom and Cherrie Gardner
Cloudland, Georgia

"My husband and I were looking through a book about birds, and he decided to try to make a copy of one of the birds he saw," says Cherrie Gardner. "We got into a friendly competition as to who could duplicate one of the birds most closely. He made the Arctic tern, and I made the red-crested cardinal."

Materials

For each: 1 English walnut
Paintbrush
Aleene's Designer Tacky Glue™
5" x 8" piece white posterboard
2 (³⁄₁₆") black beads
½" x 1" magnetic strip
For Arctic tern: Aleene's Premium-Coat™
　Acrylic Paint: Medium Grey
1 (1") pom-pom each: black, white
Red posterboard scrap
1 red chenille stem
For red-crested cardinal: Aleene's Premium-
　Coat™ Acrylic Paints: White, True Red, True
　Grey, Black
1 (1") red pom-pom
Yellow posterboard scrap
2" length ¾"-wide red ribbon

Directions

1 **For Arctic tern,** paint walnut Medium Grey. Let dry. Cut each pom-pom in half. Glue flat sides of 1 black half and 1 white half together to form head (see photo). Referring to photo, glue head, white half down, to 1 end of walnut. Let dry.

2 From white posterboard, cut 4" x 5" piece. Paint both sides Medium Grey. Let dry. Transfer patterns to painted posterboard and cut 2 wings and 1 tail. Slightly bend each wing along dotted line to shape. Dab glue along inside of curves. Place wings ³⁄₈" behind head on walnut, crossing wings over back of walnut. Dab glue on widest part of tail. Glue tail approximately ⁵⁄₈" behind head on walnut, centering under wings. Bend tail slightly upward. Let dry. Transfer beak patterns to red posterboard and cut out. Slightly bend each along dotted line to shape. Glue small beak to top edge of white pom-pom and large beak to bottom edge of black pom-pom (see photo). Let dry. Glue black beads in place for eyes. Let dry.

3 Cut 2 (3") lengths from chenille stem. Using scissors, trim fuzz from chenille stem. To make legs, referring to photo, curl ½" of 1 end of each chenille stem length into small circle. To make feet, leaving ¾" length extending from each circle, bend remainder of each chenille stem length at 90° angle. Then bend opposite end of each chenille stem length back ¼". Repeat, bending remainder of each chenille stem length back and forth ¼" until you form 3 toes. Glue circular

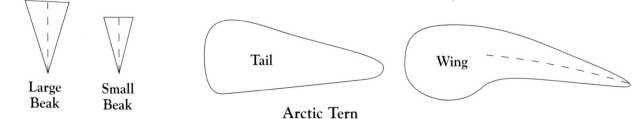

Large Beak　Small Beak　Tail　Wing

Arctic Tern

end of each leg to bottom of walnut (see photo). Let dry. Glue nonmagnetic side of magnetic strip to bird, with half of magnet on 1 wing and other half on walnut. Let dry.

4 **For red-crested cardinal,** paint entire walnut White. Let dry. At point of walnut, use True Red to paint diamond shape, extending the corners ⅝" behind point of walnut (see photo). Using True Grey, paint across half of walnut, extending ⅛" below rim of walnut and ⅛" from red diamond (see photo). Let dry.

5 For head, glue red pom-pom onto red diamond area (see photo). Let dry. Cut 4" square

from white posterboard and paint both sides with True Grey. Let dry. Transfer patterns and cut 2 wings and 1 tail. Slightly bend tail up ¼" from short edge. Glue bent ¼" of tail ¾" behind head. Let dry. Using Black, paint wide end of tail. Let dry. Glue wings in place (see photo). Let dry.

6 Transfer beak patterns to yellow posterboard and cut out. Glue small beak to pom-pom ⁵⁄₁₆" above walnut. Glue large beak above small beak. Let dry. Glue black beads in place for eyes. Roll ribbon into cone shape and glue. Let dry. Cut off bottom of cone, angling slightly. Glue cone to top of head. Glue nonmagnetic side of magnetic strip to bottom of bird. Let dry.

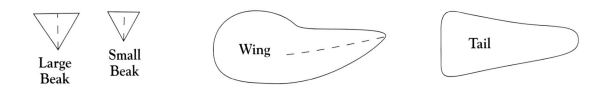

Large Beak   Small Beak   Wing   Tail

Red-crested Cardinal

Puppy Memo Holder

by Patricia LoPinto
Spring Hill, Florida

"One day while I was playing around with wooden shapes and clothespins, I realized that by combining them, I could make animals," says Patricia LoPinto. "The clothespins would be the feet that could hold memos. After trying several different designs, I came up with the puppies."

Materials

Wooden pieces: 3 (2¼"-long) ovals, 6 (⅞"-long) ovals, 6 (1½"-long) teardrops, 6 (¾"-diameter) circles, 3 (⅜"-diameter) circles, 3 (⅞"-long) teardrops, 3 (½" x 8") slats, 2 (½" x 5¼") slats
8 wooden spring-type clothespins
Aleene's Premium-Coat™ Acrylic Paints: Burnt Umber, Dusty Beige, Black, True Red
Paintbrush
Aleene's Designer Tacky Glue™
6 wiggle eyes
Aleene's Right-On Finish™
Aleene's Fusible Web™
Felt: tan, beige, black, red
Posterboard scraps
¼"-diameter round acrylic jewels in assorted colors
1 red chenille stem

Directions

1 Paint 2¼" ovals, 1½" teardrops, and handle area above spring of each clothespin Burnt Umber (see photo). Let dry. Paint ⅞" ovals, ¾"-diameter circles, and area below spring of each clothespin Dusty Beige. Let dry. Paint ⅜" circles Black. Paint ⅞" teardrops and all slats True Red. Let dry. Referring to **Diagram,** glue wooden ovals, teardrops, and circles together to form 3 puppy heads. Glue 2 wiggle eyes in place on each puppy. Let dry. Referring to photo, glue slats together to form holder base. Let dry. Apply 1 or 2 coats of Right-On Finish to each puppy head and base, letting dry between coats.

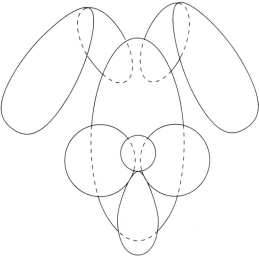

Diagram

2 Fuse web onto tan, beige, and black felt. Transfer patterns to felt and cut 6 bodies from tan, 3 tummies from beige, and 3 collars from black. Transfer pattern to posterboard scraps and cut 3 bodies, omitting legs and cutting just inside marked line. Fuse 1 felt body onto each side of 1 posterboard body. Repeat with remaining felt and posterboard bodies. Fuse 1 tummy and 1 collar in place on each body (see photo). Glue 1 head to each body. With handles pointing up, glue 2 clothespins to each body for feet. Glue acrylic jewels to each collar. Let dry.

3 Referring to photo for positioning, glue puppies to base. Let dry. For hanger, cut 2 (2") lengths of chenille stem. Bend each length in half to form a loop. Glue ends of 1 bent stem to back of top horizontal slat behind 1 vertical slat. Repeat with remaining bent stem, gluing to opposite side. Cut 3 (½" x 8") strips from red felt. Glue 1 felt strip to back of each horizontal slat, covering ends of chenille stems on top slat. Let dry.

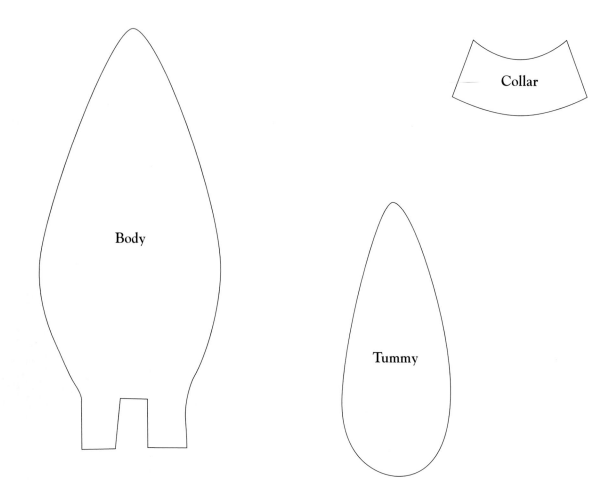

Collar

Body

Tummy

Butterfly Puppet

by Janice Brown
Hollister, California

"My daughter Audra was learning about caterpillars and butterflies at school," says Janice Brown. *"Using an old sock and felt pens, she made a sock puppet caterpillar. The next day she wanted me to turn the caterpillar into a butterfly. My son Josh thought of using Velcro to attach the wings so that they can come off and on!"*

Materials

1 green child's sock
Rolled-up newspaper
Aleene's Jewel-It™ Glue
Wiggle eyes
Assorted dimensional fabric paints
9" x 12" piece yellow felt
Pinking sheers
Assorted acrylic jewels
1 large yellow chenille stem
Aleene's Designer Tacky Glue™
Clothespins
1" x 2" piece Velcro

Directions

1 Pull sock over newspaper roll. Heel of sock is underside of puppet. Using Jewel-It Glue, glue wiggle eyes to toe portion of sock. Using dimensional paints, paint mouth and embellish body as desired. Let dry.

2 Fold felt in half widthwise. Transfer pattern to folded felt and cut 1 pair of wings, using pinking sheers. Referring to photo and using Jewel-It Glue, glue jewels to wings. Using dimensional paints, embellish wings as desired. Let dry.

3 For antennae, wrap each end of chenille stem around pencil to coil. Remove from pencil. Bend tip of each end back so that there are no sharp points. Referring to photo and **Diagram** for placement and using Designer Tacky Glue, glue antennae to head of caterpillar, pinching sock around chenille stem to secure. Hold in place with clothespins. Let dry.

4 Using Jewel-It Glue and referring to **Diagram** for placement, center and glue loop half of Velcro to center back of caterpillar and hook half to center underside of wings. Let dry.

Simply remove the wings to see what the butterfly looked like during its early stage of life.

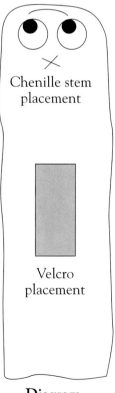

Chenille stem placement

Velcro placement

Diagram

84

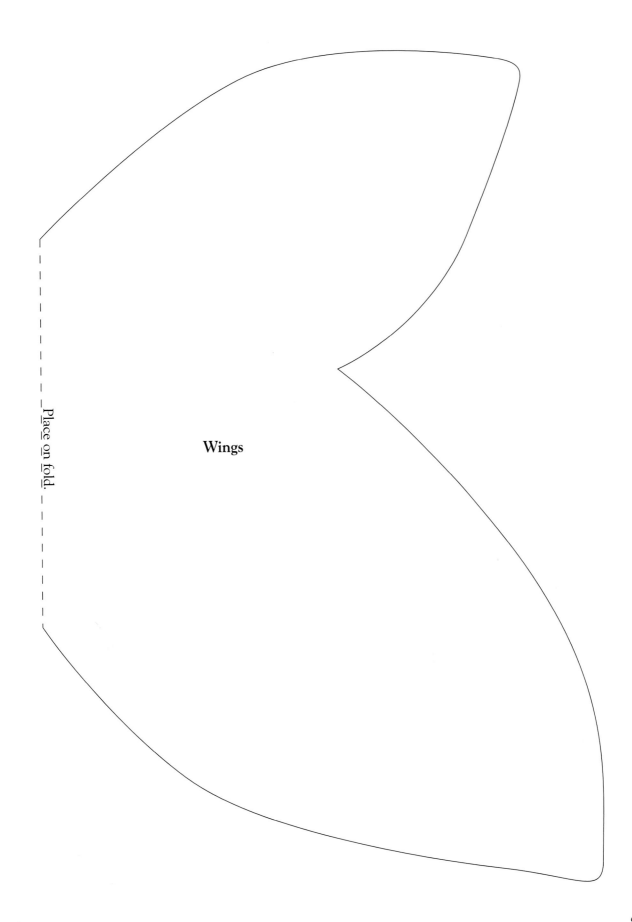

Place on fold.

Wings

Transforming Town

by Angela Kunkel Trenchik
Clovis, New Mexico

"When a pattern isn't available for what I want to make, I design my own pattern through trial and error. This was the case when my son wanted a town for his miniature cars," says Angela Trenchik. *"I created Transforming Town to be less expensive and easier to store than purchased mats. More important, it can be personalized, and the repositionable pieces promote creativity."*

Materials

Fabrics: 2 yards 60"-wide green; 1 yard 45"-wide black; ¼ yard each 45"-wide white, red, yellow, and blue

Aleene's OK to Wash-It™ Glue

3 yards 20"-wide heavyweight fusible interfacing

Dimensional fabric paints with tip: white, yellow, black, red

Aleene's Tack-It Over & Over Glue™

1½ yards 45"-wide clear vinyl

Directions

Note: To store your Transforming Town, remove pieces from green mat. Fold green mat. Store road, building, and sign pieces on vinyl to retain tackiness. You may use vinyl whole and roll it up to store, or you may cut vinyl into several smaller pieces to stack. A sweater-sized box is ideal for holding town along with miniature cars.

1 To finish edges of green fabric, turn each edge under 1" and glue, using OK to Wash-It Glue. Let dry. Referring to **Diagram,** on uncoated side of 2 yards of interfacing, draw 27 (3" x 7") straight road pieces; using patterns on pages 89–91, transfer 10 curved roads, 4 (3-way) intersections, and 3 (4-way) intersections. Do not cut out pieces. Following manufacturer's directions, fuse interfacing to back of black fabric. On remaining yard of interfacing, transfer sign patterns and draw 5" squares for buildings, adding 2" x 3" rectangle to 1 side of each building for driveway. Transfer as many signs and buildings as desired. Cut out shapes slightly larger than traced. From white fabric, cut 1 (2" x 3") rectangle for each driveway drawn on interfacing. Fuse 1 white fabric rectangle to driveway portion of each building. Fuse red,

yellow, or blue fabrics to remaining area of each building. Fuse red fabric to stop and yield patterns. Fuse yellow to remaining signs. Cut out all shapes along traced lines.

2 Using dimensional paints, paint solid white line along each long edge of road pieces. Then paint broken yellow line down center of each road piece. Paint white line across each driveway where it connects to building. Let dry. Referring to photo, label and embellish buildings and signs as desired. Let dry.

3 Apply thin coat of Tack-It Over & Over Glue to back of each road, building, and sign piece. Let dry. Position pieces as desired. Store pieces on vinyl.

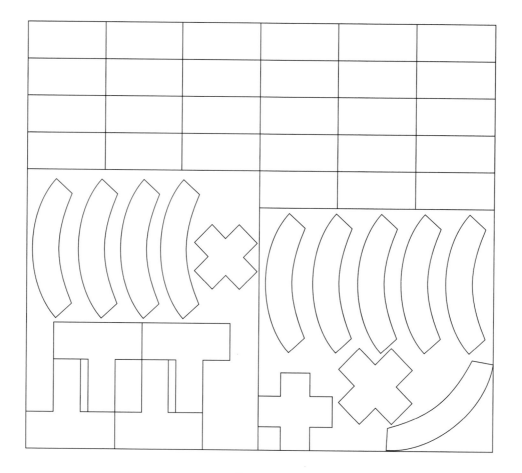

Diagram

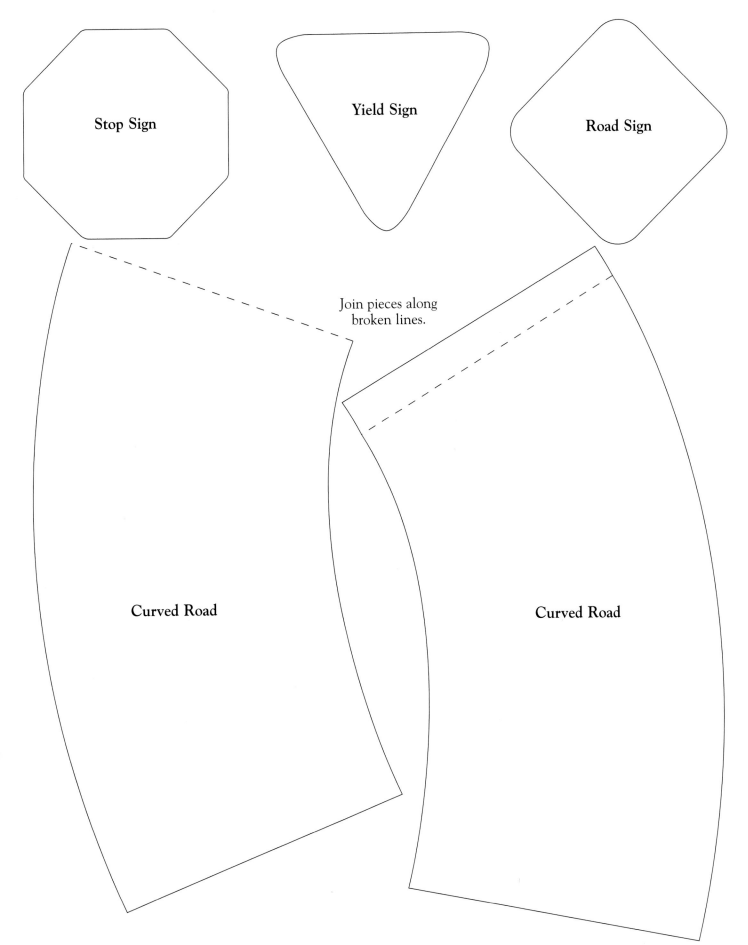

Stop Sign

Yield Sign

Road Sign

Join pieces along
broken lines.

Curved Road

Curved Road

89

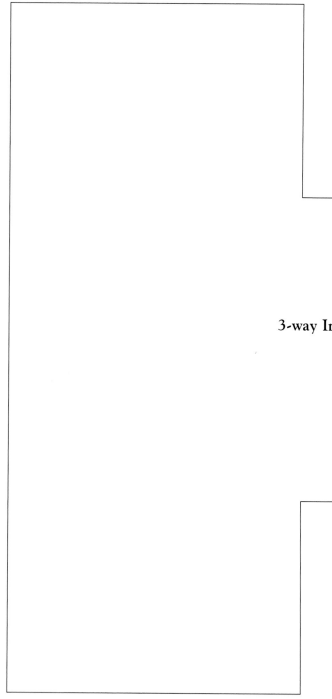

3-way Intersection

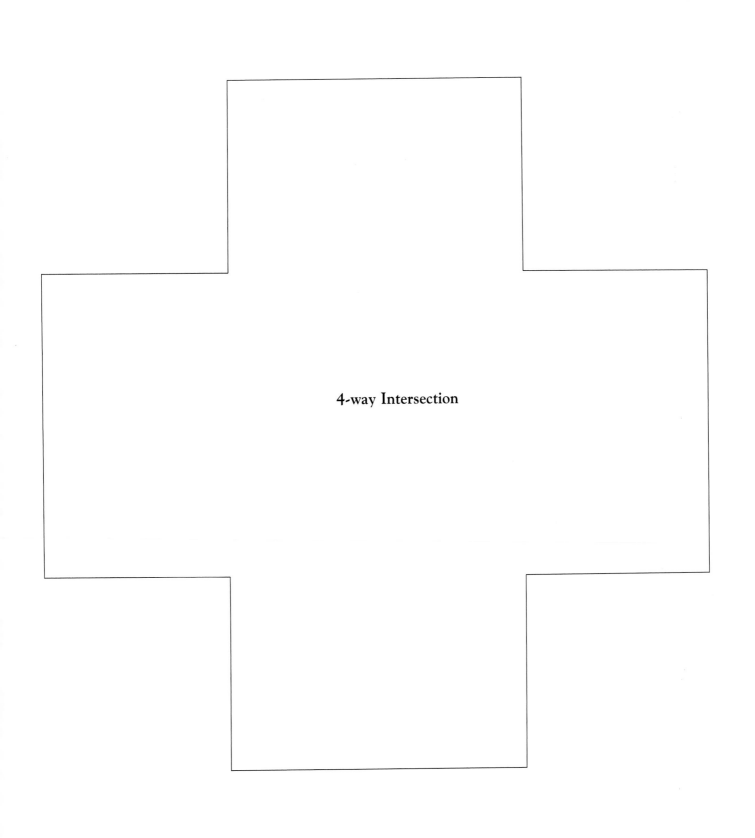

4-way Intersection

Creepy Creatures

by Heather Sellers
Sacramento, California

"Embellish your child's clothes with these bugs or let your child give them to friends or classmates," says Heather Sellers. *"You can draw your creatures freehand or follow a pattern."*

Materials

Aleene's Opake Shrink-It™ Plastic
Puffy fabric paints in variety of colors
Aleene's Tack-It Over & Over Glue™

Directions

1 To make each creature, place Shrink-It on top of pattern. Using desired color of puffy paint, trace pattern. Layer paints, making dots and lines and placing 1 color on top of another.

2 Let dry for several days. When completely dry, peel from Shrink-It. (Creature should easily peel off Shrink-It. If not, let paint dry longer.) Apply Tack-It Over & Over Glue to back of each creature. Let dry.

Creature

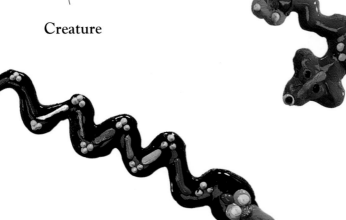

Paper Clip Clothes Hanger Jewelry

by Gina Dice
Rowland Heights, California

"The inspiration for my project came from my passion to create and to design kids' crafts for my daughters and the Girl Scout troop I lead," says Gina Dice.

Materials

For each: Aleene's Opake Shrink-It™ Plastic
Fine-grade sandpaper
Fine-tip permanent black marker
Colored pencils
¼"-diameter hole punch
Aleene's Baking Board or nonstick cookie sheet
   sprinkled with baby powder
Needlenose pliers
Colored paper clips
13 (4-mm) jump rings
For necklace: 20"-length white satin cording
Assorted pony beads
For 1 pair earrings: 2 fishhook earrings

Directions

1 Sand 1 side of each piece of Shrink-It so that markings will adhere. Be sure to thoroughly sand both vertically and horizontally. Using patterns on page 96 and black marker, trace 3 dresses for necklace and 1 shirt and 1 pair of shorts for earrings on sanded side of Shrink-It. (Marker ink may run on sanded surface; runs will shrink and disappear during baking.) Referring to photo, use colored pencils to color designs as desired. (Remember that colors will be more intense after shrinking.) Cut out designs and punch holes where indicated on patterns.

Preheat toaster oven or conventional oven to 275° to 300°. Place each design on room-temperature baking board and bake in oven. Edges should begin to curl within 25 seconds; if not, increase temperature slightly. If edges begin to curl as soon as designs are put in oven, reduce temperature. After about 1 minute, designs will lie flat. Remove designs from oven. Let cool.

2 Using pliers and referring to photo, attach 1 jump ring each to top loop of 3 clothes hangers. In same manner, attach 1 jump ring to each hole in each clothes design. Referring to photo, attach 1 dress to bottom of each clothes hanger that has a jump ring attached to top loop. Attach shirt and shorts to bottom of remaining clothes hangers.

3 **For necklace,** thread 1 dress on satin cording through jump ring on clothes hanger. Referring to photo, thread pony beads on each side of design; thread remaining 2 dresses and pony beads onto cording. Knot ends of cording.

4 **For earrings,** use pliers to attach shirt hanger to 1 fishhook earring by loop in clothes hanger. Repeat to attach shorts hanger to remaining fishhook earring.

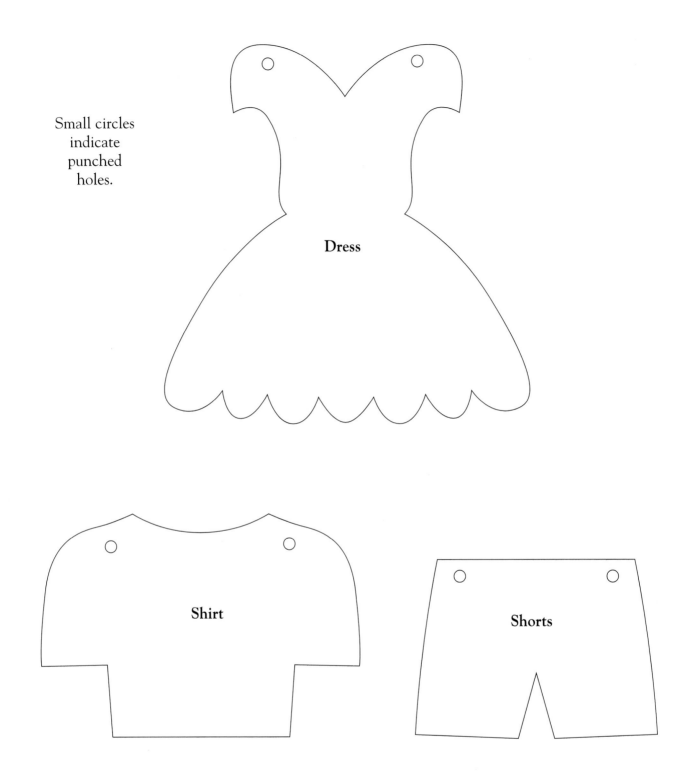

Small circles
indicate
punched
holes.

Dress

Shirt

Shorts

Dress-up Doll Sweatshirt

by Sandy Allen
Brownsburg, Indiana

"I was thinking of my seven-year-old niece when I made this sweatshirt," says Sandy Allen. "She's not very interested in dolls, but she has a mind for clothes! She has really enjoyed putting together outfits for the doll on her sweatshirt."

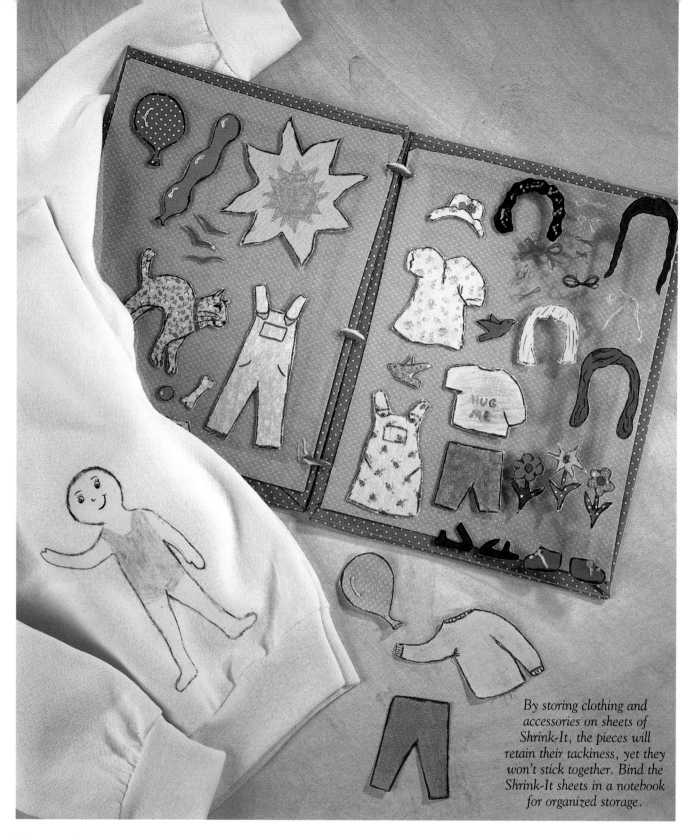

By storing clothing and accessories on sheets of Shrink-It, the pieces will retain their tackiness, yet they won't stick together. Bind the Shrink-It sheets in a notebook for organized storage.

Materials

Sweatshirt

Fabric scraps: flesh color for doll, variety of colors for clothes and accessories, muslin, desired color or print for covering storage notebook (optional)

Aleene's Fusible Web™

Embroidery floss for hair bows

Dimensional fabric paints with tip in desired colors

Aleene's Tack-It Over & Over Glue™

Aleene's Shrink-It™ Plastic

2 (8½" x 11") cardboard pieces (optional)

Hole punch (optional)

Yarn (optional)

Directions

1 Wash and dry sweatshirt and fabrics; do not use fabric softener in washer or dryer. Transfer doll pattern to fusible web. Fuse doll pattern to wrong side of flesh-colored fabric. Cut out. Remove paper backing and fuse doll onto bottom front of sweatshirt (see photo).

2 Transfer remaining patterns onto fusible web. Cut out slightly larger than traced. Fuse patterns to wrong side of desired fabric scraps. Cut out along traced lines. Remove paper backing and fuse each piece to muslin for added strength. Cut out. For hair bows, tie lengths of embroidery floss into bows. Attach length of embroidery floss to balloon for string.

Doll

3 Using fabric paints, outline doll and paint face and underwear on doll. Embellish remaining pieces as desired. Let dry.

4 Apply Tack-It Over & Over Glue to muslin side of each piece. Apply small amount of Tack-It Over & Over Glue to 1 side of hair bows. Let dry. Place wardrobe and accessories on sheets of Shrink-It when not in use.

5 If desired, make notebook to store wardrobe by fusing fabric to 2 (8½" x 11") pieces of cardboard. Punch 3 holes in cardboard pieces and in sheets of Shrink-It. Sandwich Shrink-It pages between fused cardboard pieces. Using yarn, lace notebook together.

Honorable Mention

Travel Tic-tac-toe

by Kimberly Owens
Baytown, Texas

"As a preschool teacher, I often make games to use in my classroom," says Kimberly Owens. "I like this version of tic-tac-toe because it is flexible and durable."

Materials (for 1 game)
10"-diameter circle Aleene's Fusible Web™
2 (11") squares fabric
Pinking shears
Hole punch
2 (6½") lengths each ⅜"-wide ribbon in
    2 different colors
Aleene's Stop Fraying Glue™
Aleene's OK to Wash-It™ Glue
37" length cotton cording
Fun Foam in 2 colors

Directions
1 Center and fuse web circle on wrong side of 1 fabric piece. Trim excess fabric. Remove paper backing. Center and fuse on wrong side of remaining fabric piece. Trim along edge of circle, using pinking shears.

2 For placement of holes, mark 24 evenly spaced dots around circle, ½" from edge. Using hole punch, punch holes in circle at marked dots.

3 Apply Stop Fraying Glue to cut ends of ribbon lengths. Let dry. Using OK to Wash-It Glue, center and glue ribbons in grid on 1 side of circle (see photo). For drawstring, thread cotton cording through holes, starting on side of circle without grid. Knot free ends of cording.

4 For playing pieces, transfer desired pattern to 1 color of foam and cut 5. Transfer same pattern to remaining color of foam and cut 5. To prepare game for traveling, place playing pieces in center of circle and pull drawstring, enclosing playing pieces in resulting pouch.

Heart

Star

Crafty Home Decorating

Barbara Matthiessen
Port Orchard, Washington

"Affordability, style, versatility, and easy application were my goals when designing this window treatment," says Barbara Matthiessen. *"To accomplish these I wanted to use inexpensive materials I had on hand. I decided upon brown grocery bags, since they are free, have a pleasing texture, and are like a blank canvas waiting to be covered with any design."*

Materials
¾"-wide curtain rod to fit window
Brown grocery bags
Aleene's Designer Tacky Glue™
Aleene's Fusible Web™
Fabric scraps: gold, black, green
Fine-tip permanent black marker
1¼"-wide craft ribbon in length equal to 1½
    times curtain rod length

Directions

1 Mount curtain rod to window as desired. To determine necessary finished length of valance, measure distance between curtain rod mounting brackets. Multiply finished length by 1½ to determine working length of valance.

2 Cut open 1 grocery bag to make 1 flat sheet of paper. Cut enough 12"-wide strips to equal working length of valance, using additional paper bags as needed. With printed sides up, overlap 12" ends of strips slightly and glue together. Smooth and flatten seams. Let dry.

3 To make casing, repeat Step 2, using 3"-wide strips. Referring to **Diagram,** on wrong (printed) side of 12"-wide joined piece, measure and mark 2" from top across length. On wrong (printed) side of 3"-wide joined piece, apply glue along each long edge. Aligning top long edge of 3"-wide joined piece with marked line, glue 3"-wide joined piece to wrong side of 12"-wide joined piece, making sure to leave short ends unglued and open. Smooth glued areas. Let dry.

4 For every 10" of working length of valance, you will need 1 sunflower, 1 flower center,

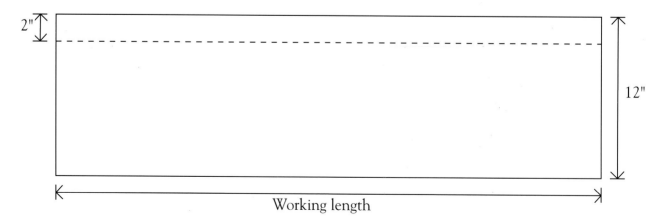

Working length

Diagram

Grocery Bag Valance

1 leaf, and 1 stem. Transfer sunflower, flower center, leaf, and stem patterns on page 22 to fusible web required number of times. Cut out slightly beyond marked solid lines. Fuse shapes to wrong side of fabrics as follows: sunflowers to gold, centers to black, and leaves and stems to green. Cut out along marked solid lines.

5 For placement guide, on right side of 12"-wide joined piece, use pencil to lightly mark every 10" along length. Remove paper backing and position designs at marks. Bottom edge of each sunflower should be 3" from bottom edge of

paper. Place 1 center on each sunflower, 1 stem under side edges of sunflowers, and end of 1 leaf under top edge of each stem. Fuse in place.

6 Using black marker, draw stitch marks on designs as shown on pattern pieces. Glue ribbon to lower edge of valance, aligning bottom edge of ribbon with bottom edge of paper. Let dry. Using black marker and referring to photo, draw vertical stitch marks every ½" along top edge of ribbon. Carefully insert curtain rod through casing to hang. Mold paper into soft folds that accent sunflowers.

Sunflower

Flower Center

Leaf

Stem

22

Basket Weave Frame

by Linda Struble of 'Artfelt Designs
Wolfeboro, New Hampshire

"Ever since I can remember, I've loved making things," says Linda Struble. "When I was a teen, Mom would encourage me to cook or to bake, but I always wanted to be in the garage with my dad, building something. I would still rather build than cook! I think that is one reason I like the burnt bag technique I used for this frame. I like working with metals, and you can achieve a metallic look with this method."

Materials

2 (8" x 9") pieces cardboard
Brown grocery bags
Aleene's Designer Tacky Glue™
3" square cardboard squeegee
Craft knife
8" length paper twist
Aleene's Premium-Coat™ Acrylic Paints: Copper,
    True Turquoise
Sea sponge
Desired photo

Directions

1 Center opening on 1 (8" x 9") cardboard piece to fit photo. Cut out. From brown bag, cut 1 (10" x 12") piece and 50 (½" x 14") strips. Referring to **Diagram,** dab glue on short ends of 10" x 12" piece. Lay 20 strips side by side across 10" x 12" piece, allowing ends of strips to extend beyond ends of paper. Let dry. Using remaining strips, weave across glued strips, making sure to push strips close together as you work. Fold ends of strips to back of 10" x 12" piece and glue. Let dry.

2 Squeegee glue on 1 side of 8" x 9" cardboard piece with opening. Center cardboard piece, glue side down, on nonwoven side of 10" x 12" woven brown bag piece and press in place. Fold excess brown bag to back of cardboard and glue. Let dry. To make frame opening, using craft knife and working from back of frame, cut an X across weave, cutting from top corners to opposite bottom corners of opening in cardboard. Fold excess brown bag to inside and glue. Let dry.

3 Spread fairly thick layer of glue on basket weave. While glue is still wet, hold design, glue side down, directly over candle flame. Hold design as close to flame as possible but don't snuff out candle. Move design around over flame until glue is black and sooty. (Burning process takes about 1½ to 2 minutes and produces a little smoke.) Using scrap of fabric, gently wipe off soot and mold soft glue, slightly ruffling surface. Let dry. For frame back, from brown bag, cut 1 (8" x 9") piece and 2 pieces slightly larger than remaining 8" x 9" cardboard piece. Layer and glue larger brown bag pieces to 1 side of remaining cardboard piece, folding excess brown bag to back and gluing in place. Glue 8" x 9" brown bag piece to remaining side of cardboard piece. Repeat burning process to burn both sides of nonwoven frame back and paper twist length. Sponge-paint each burned design with Copper. Let dry. Repeat to sponge-paint each with True Turquoise. Let dry.

4 For hanger, glue each short end of paper twist to back of frame back, approximately 2½" from top edge. Let dry. Apply glue to 3 edges of woven frame front, leaving 1 edge unglued for inserting photo. Glue woven frame front to nonwoven frame back. Let dry. Insert photo.

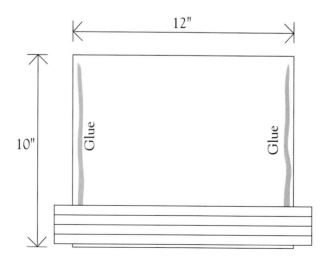

Diagram

Jeweled Leaf Box

by Sheri L. Bendorf, SCD
La Vista, Nebraska

"Nature provides fascinating design inspiration," says Sheri Bendorf. "For this project a blemish on a leaf and a lowly beetle became visual poetry. My appreciation of precious jewels inspired the materials I chose."

Materials

4½" papier-mâché heart-shaped box
Aleene's Premium-Coat™ Acrylic Paints: Deep
    Green, Black, Gold
Sponge brush
Waxed paper
Sea sponge
Paper towel
Acrylic jewels: 1 (18-mm x 24-mm) dark coral
    oval cabochon, 1 (7-mm) gold metallic round
    cabochon, 1 (8-mm) topaz round faceted
Aleene's Jewel-It™ Glue
Aleene's 3-D Foiling™ Glue
Cellophane tape
Gold press-and-peel craft foil
Small paintbrush
Green Bead Easy™ glass beads without holes
Clean dishpan
Aleene's Gloss Right-On Finish™

Directions

1 Using pencil, transfer leaf overhang patterns to sides of box lid, matching dip end of each pattern with dip in heart. Brush 1 coat of Deep Green paint onto top of lid. Referring to pattern, paint designated areas of each leaf overhang Deep Green. Let dry. (Don't worry if you paint over pencil lines. They are only painting guidelines.) Paint box and remainder of box lid Black, including insides. Let dry. Pour small amount of Gold onto piece of waxed paper. Dip sea sponge into puddle of Gold. Blot excess paint on paper towel. Lightly sponge-paint over all black areas of box. Let dry.

2 Transfer leaf pattern, including bug and blemish, to top of lid. If necessary, retransfer leaf overhang patterns to sides of lid, positioning patterns as in Step 1. Apply Jewel-It Glue to back of each jewel. Referring to photo and pattern, glue each jewel in place. Let dry.

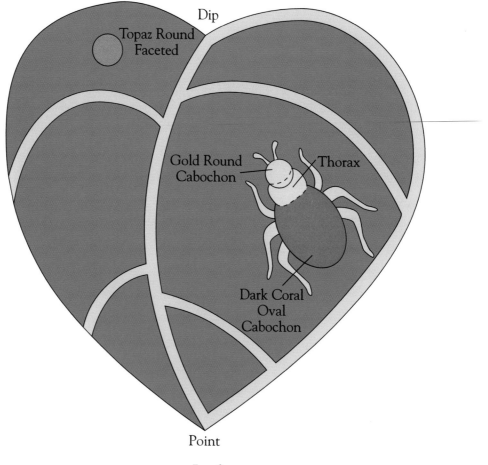

Leaf

26

3 Referring to patterns, trace vein lines of leaf and leaf overhang with 3-D Foiling Glue. Then wrap piece of cellophane tape around 3-D Foiling Glue bottle tip, positioning tape at angle and winding tape around to form cone. Cut off tip of tape to make fine point about 1/16" in diameter for glue bottle. Turn bottle upside down and tap to release air from tip before use. Trace bug legs, squeezing with varying amounts of pressure to create thick and thin areas of legs. Trace antennae. For thorax, cut cellophane tip to make approximate 1/8"-diameter tip. Fill in thorax area, using 2 to 3 layers of glue. Wait several hours between layers to form plump thorax. Let glue dry for about 24 hours. (Glue will be opaque and sticky when dry. Glue must be thoroughly dry before foil is applied.)

4 To apply gold foil, lay foil dull side down on top of glue lines. Using fingers, gently but firmly press foil onto glue, completely covering glue with foil. Be sure to press foil into crevices. Peel away foil paper. If any part of glue lines is not covered, reapply foil as needed.

5 Working on small area at a time and using small paintbrush, apply thin layer of Jewel-It Glue to green section of box lid. Holding box lid over dishpan, pour green glass beads onto glue-covered area. Press beads into glue, using your finger. Shake off excess beads into dishpan. Repeat bead-applying process several times to fill in any gaps. Then repeat on remainder of designated areas of box lid. Let dry.

6 Apply 1 coat of Right-On Finish to beaded areas. Let dry. Apply 2 coats of Right-On Finish to foiled areas, letting dry between coats. Do not seal black painted areas.

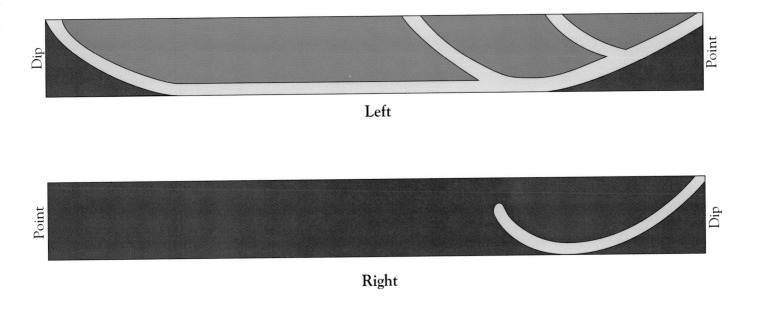

Left

Right

Leaf Overhangs

27

Southwestern Place Mat

by Tam Hutchison
Dunning, Nebraska

"The idea for this project came to me as I was trying to figure out how I could recycle my husband's jeans after I was unable to patch them any longer," says Tam Hutchison. "A set of these denim place mats is great for those who enjoy country decor."

Materials (for 2 place mats)

1 pair worn-out adult-sized jeans
Thread to match
Pop-up craft sponges
Aleene's Premium-Coat™ Acrylic Paints: True
    Red, Black
Aleene's Enhancers™ Textile Medium
2 paper plates
Waxed paper
Paper towel
Dimensional fabric paints with tip: gold glitter,
    white, black
2 bandannas

Directions

1 Wash and dry jeans; do not use fabric softener in washer or dryer. Cut along inseam of each leg. Cut 14"-long panels from each leg. Using medium-width zigzag, join panels along 14" edges. For each place mat, cut 1 (14" x 20") section from joined panels. Staystitch ⅝" from edges of each mat and then stitch again ⅛" from edges.

2 For each mat, cut out 1 back pocket, adding ⅝" to all edges. Referring to photo, position pocket about ¾" from bottom and right-hand edges of place mat. Machine-stitch pocket in place, ⅛" from pocket edge.

3 Wash place mat 2 to 3 times; do not use fabric softener in washer or dryer. Tumble partially dry at medium temperature. Remove while slightly damp. Trim raveled edges and press.

4 Transfer boot top, boot bottom, and cactus patterns to sponges and cut out. Place each sponge into water to expand and wring out excess water. Using separate paper plate for each color of acrylic paint, mix equal parts textile medium and paint. Pour small puddle of each mixed paint onto waxed paper. Dip cactus sponge into True Red paint and blot excess paint on paper towel. Referring to photo, press sponge onto place mat as desired, reloading sponge with paint after each use. Repeat to sponge-paint boots, using True Red for boot tops and Black for boot bottoms. Let dry. Referring to photo and using dimensional paints, embellish cacti with black designs, boots with gold spurs and white scrollwork, and background with black and white livestock brands. Let dry. Fold bandannas and insert 1 in pocket of each place mat for napkin.

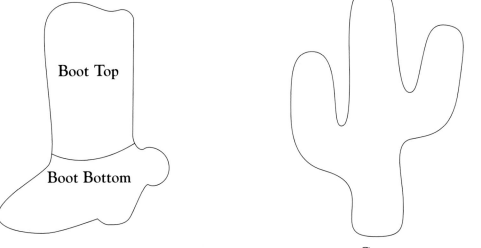

Boot Top

Boot Bottom

Cactus

Grapevine Flowerpot

by Linda J. Poulton
Little Rock, Arkansas

"I wanted to make a project with bread dough because I had never tried the technique before," says Linda Poulton. "I wanted to create something that would go with my home decor, that was different, and that would allow my creative juices to flow. So I designed this bread dough-decorated flowerpot."

Materials

4 slices white bread
Plastic cup
Aleene's Tacky Glue™
Craft stick
Waxed paper
Razor blade
Jute twine
Zip-top plastic bags
8"-diameter clay flowerpot
Aleene's Designer Tacky Glue™
Fan paintbrush
Aleene's Premium-Coat™ Acrylic Paints: Deep
    Sage, Soft Sage, Deep Fuchsia, Antique Gold
Paper towel
Aleene's Enhancers™ Matte Varnish

Directions

1 Referring to box, make bread dough, using 4 slices of white bread. To make grapes, roll dough into 12 pea-sized balls for each desired grape cluster. Place balls on waxed paper. Let dry. To make 1 leaf, pinch off small ball of dough. Flatten and mold dough into teardrop shape that is slightly thicker than a piece of paper. Make veins in leaf, using razor blade. Curl and shape leaf as desired. Repeat to make desired number of leaves. Place leaves on waxed paper. Let dry. To make 1 stem for each grape cluster, roll small amount of dough between palms to make long, thin snakelike log. Using razor blade, cut dough into desired number of ½" lengths. Place stems on waxed paper. Let dry.

2 For vine, cut the following from twine: 1 length that is 2 times circumference of pot and 1 length that is 1½ times circumference of pot. Place twine in zip-top bag. Add 1 tablespoon of Designer Tacky Glue. Thoroughly coat twine with glue. Remove short length of twine from bag, sliding fingers down length of twine to remove excess glue. Referring to photo, position twine in waves on rim of pot. Trim any excess. Remove remaining length of twine from bag. Remove excess glue as before. Referring to photo, position twine in loops and waves on side of pot. Trim any excess. Let dry. Glue individual grapes to pot to make as many clusters as desired (see photo). Top row of each cluster is made up of 2 individual grapes, next row has 4 grapes, next has 3 grapes, next has 2 grapes, and last has 1 grape. Let dry. Glue stems to top of grape clusters to connect clusters to twine vine. Let dry. Glue leaves to pot as desired. Let dry. (Rim of pot is decorated with twine vine and leaves only.)

3 Dip fan paintbrush into Deep Sage paint. Sweep paintbrush across paper towel to remove excess paint. Lightly brush paint inside rim and onto pot, leaves, vines, and stems, allowing some clay color of pot to show through. Let dry. Repeat, using small amount of Soft Sage mixed with Deep Sage. Let dry. Paint grapes Deep Fuchsia. Let dry. Repeat painting process, using Antique Gold and lightly brushing paint over entire pot surface. Let dry. Apply 2 coats of varnish to inside and outside of pot, letting dry between coats.

How to Make Bread Dough

Tear the bread into small pieces and put them in a plastic cup. Add 1 tablespoon of Tacky Glue for each slice of bread and mix with a craft stick until a coarse ball forms. Remove the ball of dough from the cup. With clean hands, knead the dough until smooth, pliable, and claylike in consistency. To color the dough, flatten the ball in your hand and make a small well in the center. Pour a small amount of paint into the well. Knead the dough in your hands until the paint is thoroughly incorporated. (Store the bread dough in a zip-top plastic bag when not in use.)

Woodland Candle Ring

by Karen M. Blonigen
South Saint Paul, Minnesota

"This past winter my longing for our cabin in the woods inspired this project," says Karen Blonigen. "I chose to make the candle ring with the burnt brown bag technique because it is so simple, yet it looks sophisticated."

Materials
Brown grocery bags
Craft knife
Aleene's Tacky Glue™
3" square cardboard squeegee
18-gauge florist's wire: 2" length, 1½" length
Needlenose pliers
Muslin scrap
Aleene's Premium-Coat™ Acrylic Paints: Deep Green, Dusty Blue, White, Burnt Umber, True Red, Deep Mauve
Small sponge pieces
Clothespins
Pillar candle

Directions

1 Transfer patterns on page 34 to brown bags and cut 3 trees, 3 roofs, and 4 candle rings, extending each end of ring 3" as indicated on pattern. With edges aligned, stack and glue matching bag pieces together, using squeegee. For smoke, referring to photo, insert ¼" of 1 end of each wire between layers of chimney on roof. Let dry. Use pliers to curl free ends of wire as desired.

2 To burn each piece, spread even coat of glue on 1 side. While glue is still wet, hold design, glue side down, directly over candle flame. Hold design as close to flame as possible but don't snuff out candle. Move design around over flame until all glue is black and sooty. (Burning process takes 1½ to 2 minutes and produces a little smoke.) Using muslin scrap, gently wipe off soot and mold soft glue. Let dry overnight. Repeat to burn remaining side of each piece.

3 Sponge-paint trees and base of candle ring, using Deep Green, Dusty Blue, and White. Sponge-paint cabin, using Burnt Umber. Sponge-paint roof, using True Red and Deep Mauve. Let dry. Referring to photo, glue roof and tree in place on candle ring. Use clothespins to hold pieces in place until glue is dry. Wrap ring around pillar candle, overlapping ends to fit snugly. Remove candle. Glue overlapped ends together. Use clothespins to hold ends in place until glue is dry.

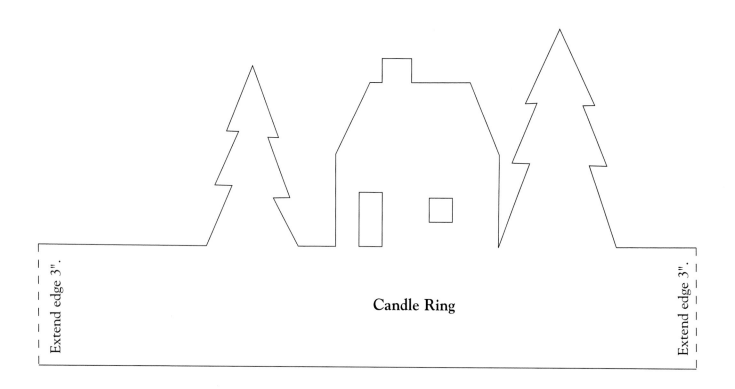

Pinecone Flowers

by Ruby L. Baker
Palo Cedro, California

"I have been artistically active all my life," says Ruby Baker. "But when I lost the vision in my left eye and partial vision in my right eye, I had to find something creative I could still do. I found some perfectly shaped pinecones and saw in my mind's eye how beautiful they could become."

Materials

Pinecones in variety of sizes and types
Cookie sheet
Handsaw or pruning shears
Wire cutters
Aleene's Tacky Glue™
Ice pick
Candle
14-gauge florist's wire
Paintbrushes: 1"-wide, small
White spray primer
Spray paints in desired colors
Aleene's Premium-Coat™ Acrylic Paints in
    shades slightly darker than spray paints
Cornmeal
Flour
Plastic cup
Green florist's tape
Clear acrylic spray sealer

Directions

1 Place pinecones on cookie sheet and bake in 200° oven for 1 hour to kill bugs and to dry out pinecones. Saw or cut pinecones into sections, according to sizes of flowers desired. If necessary, trim pinecone sections with wire cutters to shape into flowers. (Use Tacky Glue to reattach any pinecone parts that break or fall off.) Turn pinecone flowers upside down. Heat ice pick in candle flame. Carefully burn ⅔"-deep hole in bottom center of each pinecone flower, using heated ice pick. For stems, cut desired lengths of florist's wire. Squirt Tacky Glue into hole in bottom of each pinecone flower. Insert 1 length of wire into each hole. Let dry.

2 Mix 1 part Tacky Glue with 2 parts water. Working on 1 pinecone flower at a time, brush light coat of glue mixture onto flower. Let dry. Spray pinecone flower with primer. Let dry. Spray flower with 2 coats of desired color of paint, letting dry between coats. Using complementary acrylic paint, paint edges and tips of pinecone flower to shade.

3 For flowers with centers, combine 3 tablespoons of cornmeal, 3 tablespoons of Tacky Glue, and 1 tablespoon of flour in plastic cup. Mix until claylike in consistency. Roll and mold mixture into desired flower center shapes. Press 1 in center of each selected pinecone flower. Let dry overnight. Using acrylic paints, paint flower centers in desired colors.

4 For each pinecone flower, wrap wire stem with florist's tape. Spray flower with acrylic sealer. Let dry. Arrange pinecone flowers as desired.

36

Honorable Mention

Terra-cotta Cow Pot

by Vanessa J. Mackenzie
Vancouver, BC, Canada

"I got the idea for making the cow when I was decorating plant pots for Christmas presents," says Vanessa Mackenzie. "I started by painting a pot to look like a horse for a friend of mine. Then I decided I could use the idea to make any hoofed animal. I had several cow motif objects in my kitchen, so I painted a cow for myself."

This whimsical cow becomes truly animated with the addition of small pot hooves and a braided tail.

Materials
Clay pots: 4 (2"-diameter), 1 (6½"-diameter)
Aleene's Enhancers™ All-Purpose Primer
Paintbrushes
Aleene's Premium-Coat™ Acrylic Paints: White, Black, Medium Blue, Beige, Medium Fuchsia
Aleene's Enhancers™ Matte Varnish
Aleene's Designer Tacky Glue™
1" cowbell
6" length black wavy synthetic hair*
8" length ⅛"-wide blue satin ribbon
　*Note: Wavy hair is sold in braided lengths. Do not unbraid. Tie off braid after cutting to prevent remaining hair from unbraiding.

Directions
1 Paint outside of each pot with 1 coat of primer. Let dry. Paint outside of each 2"-diameter pot White. Let dry. Paint rim of each 2"-diameter pot Black. Let dry.

2 Transfer cow head pattern to 6½"-diameter pot. Draw line around pot from 1 side of head to other side of head for cow body. Paint sky above cow Medium Blue. Paint White highlights in sky. Let dry. Paint cow White. Let dry. Using Black, outline cow body and head and paint spots on cow body. Let dry. Paint horns Beige and nose Medium Fuchsia. Let dry. Paint nostrils and eyes Black. Let dry.

3 Apply 2 coats of varnish to inside and outside of each pot, letting dry between coats.

4 Turn 2"-diameter pots upside down. Referring to photo, glue bottom of each 2"-diameter pot to bottom of 6½"-diameter pot for hooves. Let dry. Glue cowbell to bottom of 6½"-diameter pot below cow head. Dip 1 end of braided wavy hair length into glue. Let dry. Attach glue-covered end to back of cow for tail (see photo). Let dry. Tie ribbon in bow about 1" from free end of tail. Unbraid tail from bow to end.

Cow Head

Birdhouse Window Treatment

by Sharon Erickson
Willmar, Minnesota

"In searching for a quick, easy, inexpensive, and unique window treatment for a patio door and two windows, I came up with the birdhouse curtain hooks," says Sharon Erickson. "The perches are used to hold up the valance, which is made from purchased table runners."

Materials

Wooden birdhouse fronts with perches
Spray primer
Aleene's Premium-Coat™ Acrylic Paints in
    desired colors
Paintbrushes
Table runners
Grommets and grommet tool
Picture hangers

Directions

1 Spray birdhouses with primer. Let dry. Using acrylic paints, paint birdhouses. Let dry.

2 For valance, with right sides facing, machine-stitch table runners together along 1 short edge, if necessary, to achieve desired length. Install grommets along 1 long edge, spacing grommets as necessary to achieve desired look.

3 Using picture hangers, mount birdhouses on wall above window, spacing as desired. Hang valance from birdhouses by sliding grommet openings onto perches (see photo).

Iris Suncatcher

by Franka Bradley
Fort Harrison, Indiana

"My husband is a chaplin in the Army and, as a result, we move a lot," says Franka Bradley. "I came up with this project because I love stained-glass windows and wanted to find a way to create that effect but still make the stained glass removable. That way we could take it with us to our next home."

Materials

Paper napkins: pink, purple
9" x 11" piece medium-weight flexible plastic
  (available in crafts or fabric stores)
Aleene's Paper Napkin Appliqué™ Glue
¼" flat shader paintbrush
Dark gray dimensional craft paint
Aleene's 3-D Foiling™ Glue
Gold press-and-peel craft foil
Transparent-drying stained-glass paints: green,
  clear textured
Toothpicks

Directions

1 Transfer irises to paper napkins and cut 1 iris bloom each from pink and purple (see photo). Remove bottom plies of napkins to leave cutouts 1-ply thick. Center plastic on top of suncatcher pattern. Brush Napkin Appliqué Glue on plastic to cover area for 1 iris. Crumple corresponding napkin piece and then flatten it, leaving some wrinkles. Press napkin onto glue-covered area. Brush coat of Napkin Appliqué Glue on top of napkin, wrinkling paper to add texture and shaping it to fit design area. Repeat to glue remaining iris in place on plastic. Let dry.

2 Trace all lines of iris design except outer border, using dark gray dimensional paint. Let dry. Trace outer border of design with 3-D Foiling Glue. Let glue dry for about 24 hours. (Glue will be opaque and sticky when dry. Glue must be thoroughly dry before foil is applied.)

3 To apply gold foil, lay foil dull side down on top of glue lines. Using fingers, gently but firmly press foil onto glue, completely covering glue with foil. Be sure to press foil into crevices. Peel away foil paper. If any part of glue lines is not covered, reapply foil as needed.

4 Paint leaves with green transparent-drying paint, using toothpick to spread paint. In same manner, paint background area of design with clear textured transparent-drying paint. Let dry.

5 Trim excess plastic from design. Press design undecorated side down onto clean window or mirror.

Suncatcher

Snowy Forest Table Runner

by Elizabeth Smith
Westbury, New York

"On suburban Long Island it's not easy to find pretty flowering weeds that I can pick," says Elizabeth Smith. *"By the time I figure out a way to get to these beauties, they've usually been mowed! So imagine my pleasure when I spotted a pressed flower-lover's Garden of Eden in the woods next to my in-laws' home in New Hampshire! My mother-in-law and I tiptoed our way through the mounds of poison ivy to the ferns and the Queen Anne's lace. It was worth the trip because the ferns looked like miniature Christmas trees and the Queen Anne's lace resembled perfect snowflakes."*

Materials

Fern fronds
Queen Anne's lace blossoms
Phone book or flower press
13¾" x 59¾" or desired size heavyweight artist's
    canvas for table runner
Acrylic gesso
Foam paintbrush
Spray paints: light blue, medium blue-gray,
    medium green, white
Aleene's Instant Decoupage™ Glue
Aleene's Tacky Glue™
4¼ yards 1½"-wide black-and-white checked
    ribbon

Directions

1 Pick fern fronds and Queen Anne's lace blossoms. If plants are wet from rain or dew, let plants dry before picking. Place each plant between pages of phone book or in flower press. Press for 2 to 3 weeks or until completely dry.

2 Apply 2 coats of gesso to each side of canvas, letting dry between coats.

3 Referring to photo for inspiration, spray-paint right side of canvas until you achieve desired effect. Use blue and green paints for sky. Use white to highlight sky and to paint snow-covered ground. Let dry.

4 Brush coat of Decoupage Glue on canvas in desired position for first Christmas tree. Press 1 fern frond wrong side down onto glue-covered area. Gently brush coat of Decoupage Glue on top of fern frond. In same manner, glue additional fern fronds for trees and Queen Anne's lace blossoms for snowflakes onto canvas. Let dry. Brush 3 or 4 coats of Decoupage Glue on right side of canvas, letting dry between coats.

5 To bind edges of table runner, cut 2 (60¾") lengths and 2 (14¾") lengths of ribbon. (If table runner is size other than 13¾" x 59¾", cut 2 ribbon lengths 1" longer than length of runner and 2 ribbon lengths 1" longer than width of runner.) Using Tacky Glue, glue 1 (60¾") ribbon length to each long edge of runner, folding each end ½" over edge of canvas. In same manner, glue 1 (14¾") ribbon length to each short end of runner. Let dry. Brush 1 coat of Decoupage Glue over entire surface of table runner. Let dry.

Gilded Ivy Frame

by Robin D. Siepel
Fayetteville, Georgia

"As an avid recycler and crafter, I am continually looking for ways to combine the two interests," says Robin Siepel. "My mother recently had her foyer hand-painted with ivy leaves trailing over the door. Her birthday was approaching, and I was looking for a unique gift to complement her decor. I presented her with this frame made from a recycled bleach bottle. It was an instant hit!"

Materials

8" x 12" piece lightweight cardboard or mat board
Craft knife
Gold metallic wax
1 clean, dry gallon or half-gallon bleach bottle
   with label removed
Awl or sharp object to score leaf veins
Aleene's Designer Tacky Glue™
Child's watercolor kit (optional)
Acrylic matte spray sealer
Desired 3" x 5" photo

Directions

1 From cardboard or mat board, cut 2 (4½" x 6½") pieces and 1 (2" x 3") piece. For frame front, on 1 (4½" x 6½") piece, measure and mark 1" in from each edge. Using craft knife, cut out along marks to make frame opening. Using gold metallic wax and your finger, apply wax to front and edges of each cardboard piece. Let dry. Repeat to apply wax to back of cardboard pieces. Let dry.

2 Referring to **Diagram A,** cut out center section of bleach bottle. Cut down 1 side so that section will lie flat. Transfer patterns to flattened bleach bottle section and cut 26 small ivy leaves and 5 large ivy leaves. Using awl and referring to patterns, score veins on 1 side of each leaf. Apply gold metallic wax to front and back of each leaf. Let dry. Repeat to apply wax to back of each leaf. Let dry.

3 Determine whether you want vertical or horizontal frame and place leaves accordingly. Glue 1 large leaf to each corner of frame front. Glue small leaves around frame front, overlapping leaves as you work. Glue remaining large leaf to center top of frame front. Let dry.

4 For verdigris finish, using paintbrush, dab (do not brush) green paint from watercolor kit onto leaves. Let dry. Spray entire frame with acrylic sealer. Let dry. Apply glue along 3 edges of back of frame front, leaving 1 edge unglued for inserting photo. Glue frame front to remaining 4½" x 6½" cardboard piece. Let dry. For frame stand, using craft knife, score 2" x 3" cardboard piece ½" from 1 short edge to make tab. Referring to **Diagram B,** glue tab to back of frame. Let dry. Insert photo into frame.

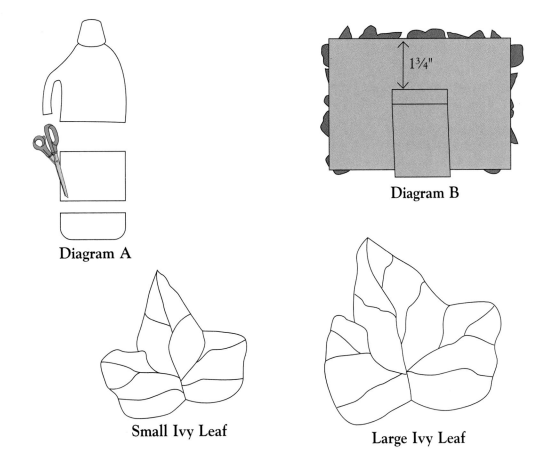

Diagram A

Diagram B

Small Ivy Leaf

Large Ivy Leaf

Faux Etched Mirror

by Angela Edele
Severance, New York

"I developed my faux etching cream because the replacement for a broken etched panel of glass in my wood stove was almost double the price of a plain glass panel," says Angela Edele. *"After much trial and error and a few disappointments, I came up with my new crafting medium. I have even made several projects using this technique with the help of three- and four-year-olds in my day care."*

Materials

Mirror
Glass cleaner
Paper towels
Purchased stencil
Aleene's Tack-It Over & Over Glue™ (optional)
Sponge brushes
Peel-and-stick vinyl shelf covering (optional)
Craft knife (optional)
Aleene's Paper Napkin Appliqué™ Glue
Cornstarch
Plastic cup
Wooden craft stick
Makeup sponge (optional)
Spray kitchen cleaner (optional)
Razor blade
Bread dough roses and leaves (optional)

Directions

Note: Faux etching cream also works well when applied to regular glass. For faux etching cream to cure, do not clean faux etched pieces for 10 days. To clean faux etched pieces, use glass cleaner and paper towels.

1 Using glass cleaner and paper towels, clean mirror and wipe dry. To prepare stencil, brush thin coat of Tack-It Over & Over Glue to back of stencil and let dry for 1 hour. Or transfer stencil to vinyl side of shelf covering and, using craft knife, cut out areas corresponding to open areas of stencil. Affix prepared stencil to surface of mirror and press to attach securely. Rub especially along edges to ensure that stencil adheres well and that edges of finished image will be well defined.

2 To make faux etching cream, combine 1 tablespoon of Napkin Appliqué Glue with 1 teaspoon of cornstarch in plastic cup. Using craft stick, mix until smooth. Using sponge brush and working quickly, lightly sweep faux etching cream back and forth across cutout areas of stencil. (Dabbing faux etching cream into cutout areas with a makeup sponge will produce a slightly different etching effect. You may want to experiment to see which look you prefer.) Carefully remove stencil. Let cream dry. Clean stencil immediately. (Tack-It Over & Over Glue may be removed from back of stencil with spray kitchen cleaner.) Use razor blade to remove any faux etching cream that bled under stencil. If desired, embellish mirror with bread dough roses and leaves (see Bread Dough Bridal Veil, page 136).

Plastic Canvas
Wind Socks

by Shirley C. Ridge
Tampa, Florida

"As an occupational therapy assistant student, I work with young people with disabilities," says Shirley Ridge. "These low-cost wind socks meet all the requirements I was looking for in a craft: Making them is fun, increases fine motor skills and hand strength, and provides a goal rather than just repetitive exercise. And choosing colors and designs calls on planning skills and imagination."

Materials

For each: Waxed paper
1-ply white paper napkins
Index card
Aleene's Paper Napkin Appliqué™ Glue
7 mesh plastic canvas, 21 squares wide x 90 squares long
Aleene's OK to Wash-It™ Glue
Clothespins
2 (22") lengths fishing line
For floral wind sock: Dimensional craft paints: yellow, green, pink
Surveyor's plastic flag ribbon: pink, yellow
For Southwestern wind sock: Dimensional craft paints: blue, purple, yellow, green, red
Surveyor's plastic flag ribbon: red, yellow

Directions

1 **For each,** cover work area with waxed paper. Unfold napkins and place single layer on waxed paper. Napkins should extend beyond edges of plastic canvas. Using index card, spread coat of Napkin Appliqué Glue over napkins. Center and press plastic canvas onto glue-covered napkins. Turn entire piece, including waxed paper, upside down onto another piece of waxed paper. Remove original piece of waxed paper and make sure napkins are adhered to plastic canvas. Let dry overnight. Trim excess napkins from edges of plastic canvas.

2 With napkin side down, referring to color chart and beginning at center of plastic canvas, transfer desired pattern to plastic canvas by squeezing designated color of dimensional paint into each square. Repeat pattern until entire strip is covered. Let dry overnight.

3 **For floral wind sock,** cut 10 (20") lengths each from pink and yellow ribbons. **For Southwestern wind sock,** cut 10 (20") lengths each from red and yellow ribbons.

Place plastic canvas wrong side up on work surface. Using OK To Wash-It Glue, glue 1 short end of each ribbon length along bottom edge of plastic canvas, alternating colors. Let dry. Squeeze line of glue along 1 short edge of plastic canvas. Overlap ends to form circle and hold with clothespins until dry. To form hanger, tie ends of 1 fishing line length to opposite sides of plastic canvas top. In same manner, tie remaining fishing line length so that top of wind sock is divided into quarters. Apply glue to knots to secure fishing line. Let dry.

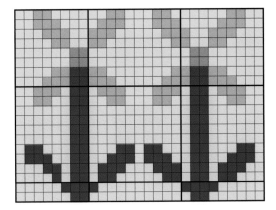

Floral

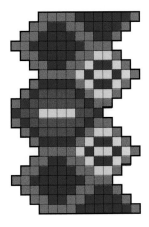

Southwestern

Decorative Switch Plates

by Marie Deatsch
Victor, New York

"The switch plate projects came about while I was in my craft studio, working with Aleene's Paper Napkin Appliqué Glue," says Marie Deatsch. "I was relaxing, waiting for a project to dry, when my gaze fell on the switch plate in the room. This is an item often overlooked in home decor. People usually only wallpaper or paint over switch plates. I chose instead to design some to match room decor and to celebrate occasions and seasons."

Materials

Decorative wrapping paper or tissue paper
Clear switch plate
Sponge paintbrush
Aleene's Reverse Collage™ Glue
Flat embellishments, such as confetti or watch
 pieces (optional)
Plain tissue paper in color to coordinate with
 decorative paper

Directions

1 Cut motifs from decorative paper. Separate
 switch plate and set back aside. Brush coat of
Reverse Collage Glue on inside of switch plate
front. If desired, sprinkle flat embellishments onto
glue. Glue cutout motifs facedown on top of
embellishments. Let dry.

2 Tear plain tissue paper into odd-shaped
 pieces. Brush coat of Reverse Collage Glue
inside of switch plate back. Press tissue paper
pieces onto glue-covered area, overlapping pieces
for added dimension. Brush another coat of
Reverse Collage Glue over tissue-covered area.
Let dry overnight. Assemble switch plate.

Switch Plate Suggestions

 To spark your creativity, here are just a few
switch plate possibilities. You can decorate
them all using the reverse collage technique.
 • Use wrapping paper with a holiday motif
to create a switch plate that celebrates special
days and changing seasons.
 • Cut out the letters of a child's name from
baby shower wrapping paper to personalize a
switch plate for a newborn's room.
 • Give a new neighbor a switch plate
accented with an area map as a welcome-to-
town gift.
 • Proudly display a child's artwork with a
switch plate decorated with one of the budding
artist's drawings.
 • Use a decorative napkin from your last
party to embellish your own switch plates.

Taper
Candle Rings

Honorable Mention

by Gail Corson Eaton
Ramona, California

"After making Christmas angels, I arranged them on tables with candles in candle holders," says Gail Eaton. "I wanted to dress up my candles with something that would complement the angels. I looked through all the stores for taper candle rings but could not find anything I liked. So I came up with my own designs."

Materials

For each: Rolling pin
Craft knife
Cookie sheet covered with aluminum foil
Aleene's Designer Tacky Glue™
Taper candle
Candle holder
For holly candle ring: Modeling compound: green, red
For rose candle ring: Modeling compound: white, desired color for roses
Aleene's Premium-Coat™ Acrylic Paint: Deep Green
Small paintbrush

Directions

1 **For each,** roll desired color of modeling compound into snakelike log. Shape log into ring that is approximate width and diameter of ring pattern.

2 **For holly candle ring,** using rolling pin, flatten portion of green modeling compound to approximately ⅛" thick. Using holly leaf pattern, cut flattened modeling compound into 18 holly leaf shapes. Using craft knife, score groove down center of each holly leaf. Roll red modeling compound into 9 small balls for holly berries. Gently press leaves onto ring, overlapping leaves and allowing them to curve gently over edge of ring. Place leaf-covered ring and berries on cookie sheet covered with foil and bake, following manufacturer's directions. Let cool. Using Tacky Glue, glue holly leaves to ring. (Baking does not adhere leaves to ring.) Glue holly berries in groups of 3 to holly leaves. Let dry.

3 **For rose candle ring,** using rolling pin, flatten portion of white modeling compound to approximately ⅛" thick. Using rose leaf pattern, cut flattened modeling compound into desired number of leaf shapes. Using craft knife, score veins on top of each leaf. To make rose, pinch off pea-sized bit of desired color of modeling compound. Squeeze pea between fingers to flatten into small, round piece the thickness of paper. For center of rose, roll flattened piece, turning top edge back slightly. Pinch off another pea-sized piece of dough and flatten as before. Press top edge back slightly to make petal. Wrap petal around center, gently pressing together at bottom. Place next petal opposite first petal and press together at bottom. Continue in same manner for total of 3 to 4 petals, overlapping edges slightly and placing subsequent petals higher on rose so that turned-back edges are even with rose center. Cut off bottom of rose. Repeat to make total of 10 to 12 roses. Place leaves, roses, and ring on cookie sheet covered with foil and bake, following manufacturer's directions. Let cool.

4 Dilute Deep Green paint with water. Paint watery coat of green paint on rose leaves. Let dry. Using Tacky Glue, glue roses to ring. Tuck rose leaves between roses and glue to ring. Let dry.

Rose Leaf

Holly Leaf

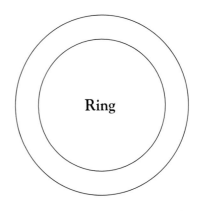

Ring

Holidays and Special Days

Moravian
Advent Star

Nancy L. Bridgers
Winston-Salem, North Carolina

"I have been a member of the Moravian Church all my life," Nancy Bridgers says. "I grew up watching my father put together a Moravian Advent Star to hang on our porch during the Advent season. Just before Christmas last year, I was in a Moravian bookstore and saw an expensive punched-tin Moravian Star. It occurred to me that, using the burnt brown bag technique, I could create a star that looked like punched tin. It turned out great, and everyone who saw it thought it was real punched tin."

Materials
Thin cardboard
Brown grocery bags
1/8"-diameter hole punch
3" square cardboard for squeegee
Aleene's Tacky Glue™
Tweezers
Candle
Soft cloth
Pewter paste paint
Aleene's Designer Tacky Glue™
Aluminum soft drink can
Toothpick
Waxed paper
Aleene's Tack-It Over & Over™ Glue
4-watt clear light bulb
Electric cord with detachable plug
Pint jar with wide mouth

Directions

1 Transfer square point and triangle point patterns on page 108 and all markings to cardboard and cut 1 of each. Using cardboard pieces as templates, transfer patterns and all markings to brown bags and cut 18 square points and 8 triangle points. Referring to pattern, label all tabs on square points. With markings to inside, fold each point along fold lines, leaving tabs unfolded. Open and flatten each point. Punch holes where indicated.

2 To burn each point, spread thick layer of Tacky Glue on unmarked side of point, using squeegee. While glue is wet, hold point (glue side down) directly over candle flame, using tweezers. Move point around over flame until entire glue area is black and sooty. (Burning process takes 1½ to 2 minutes and produces a little smoke.) Using soft cloth, gently wipe off soot. Apply pewter paste paint over burned surface, using finger. Polish paste paint with soft cloth to shine.

3 To form each point, squeeze thin line of Designer Tacky Glue along burned edge of point where indicated on marked side. Referring to **Diagram A,** refold point along fold lines and press glue-covered edge to back of opposite side. Be sure point is sharp. Let dry. Fold tabs toward burned side of point. (Be sure each point is level by setting point, tabs down, on work surface. If point is not level, adjust by cutting slightly between tabs.)

4 To assemble center of star, squeeze Designer Tacky Glue on paper side of 1 tab X on 1 square point and burned side of 1 tab O on another square point. Referring to **Diagram B,** with tab X on top, align creases of points and press together. Let dry. Repeat to glue total of 8 square points together. Let dry. Form circle with square points by gluing end tabs together in same manner. Place circle around soft drink can to shape. Let dry. Remove circle from can.

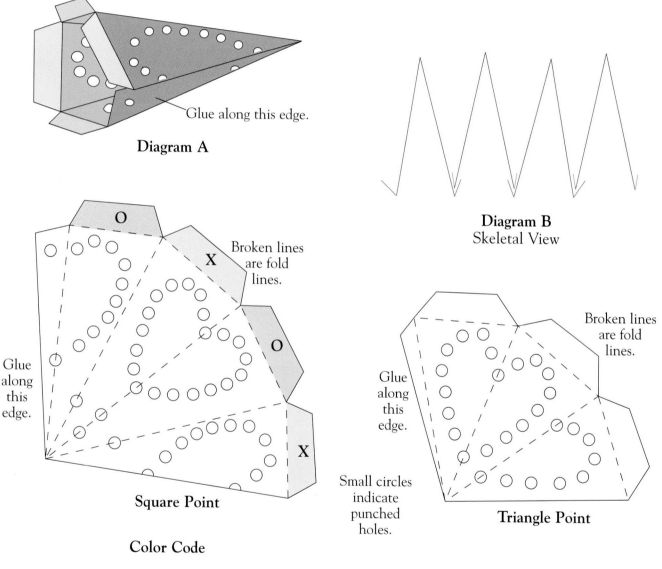

Glue along this edge.

Diagram A

Diagram B
Skeletal View

O

X

O

Broken lines are fold lines.

Glue along this edge.

X

Square Point

Broken lines are fold lines.

Glue along this edge.

Small circles indicate punched holes.

Triangle Point

Color Code

O

X

5 To assemble top of star, place 1 square point on work surface. This is center square. Matching Xs to Os on tabs and aligning creases as in Step 4, glue 1 square point to each tab of center square. Let dry. Cut tabs between each of the 4 surrounding squares **(Diagram C)**. To attach top to center, align creases and glue 4 top tabs to tab Xs of center piece. Let dry. (You should see triangular spaces between top and center pieces. You should also have 4 free tabs and 4 tabs attached to top of star.)

Squeeze line of Designer Tacky Glue on top of 1 free center tab and bottom of each tab of 1 triangle point. Aligning creases of triangle tab and free tab, place triangle in triangular space. Use toothpicks to press tabs against side of each point. Repeat to glue total of 4 triangle points between center and top of star. Let dry.

7 Pour small amount of Designer Tacky Glue on waxed paper. Let glue set until thick. Referring to **Diagram D**, align folded lines on each square tab. Apply dot of glue to 1 side of 1 tab where fold lines meet. Gently press adjoining tab into glue. Let dry. Repeat to glue all tabs together at fold line. (You should have square opening at bottom of star and triangular openings around side.) See Step 5 to glue remaining triangle points in place. Let dry.

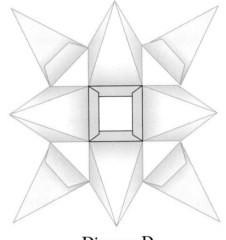

Diagram D

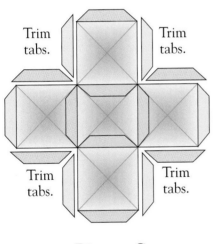

Diagram C

6 To assemble bottom of star, fold back every tab O on center piece. Aligning creases and matching Xs to Os as in Step 4, glue 1 square point to each tab X on center piece. Let dry. Referring to Step 5, cut tabs between each of 4 surrounding squares.

8 To light star, cut ¼" from tip of remaining square point. Screw light bulb tightly into socket. Remove plug from cord and insert cord through remaining square point, leaving socket ¼" above tabs. Replace plug. Using Designer Tacky Glue, glue cord to tip of point. Let dry. Place plug end of cord in pint jar until tabs of square are level with mouth of jar. Squeeze generous amount of Tack-It Over & Over Glue on all 4 tabs. Let dry. Remove cord from jar. With star upside down, align creases and insert bulb (square tabs down) to cover remaining hole. (Tack-It Over & Over Glue will allow you to change light bulb when necessary.)

Honorable Mention

Easter Sweatshirt

by Kathryn Luke-Miller
Clarks Summit, Pennsylvania

"I got the idea for this project when I saw a display of four colors of plastic wrap in a local store," says Kathryn Luke-Miller. "I had been experimenting with Aleene's Paper Napkin Appliqué Glue earlier, and it occurred to me to try appliquéing with plastic. Because of the colors of plastic wrap available, I leaned toward making an Easter sweatshirt."

Materials
White sweatshirt
Cardboard covered with waxed paper
5" x 10" piece thin cardboard
Plastic wrap: pink, green, yellow, blue
Transparent tape
Craft knife
Disappearing-ink fabric marker
Aleene's Paper Napkin Appliqué™ Glue
Paintbrush
Ultrafine iridescent glitter
Dimensional fabric paints with tip: pink, white, yellow

Directions
1 Wash and dry sweatshirt; do not use fabric softener in washer or dryer. Place cardboard covered with waxed paper inside sweatshirt.

2 Layering 1 piece at a time, wrap 5" x 10" piece of cardboard with each color of plastic wrap. Smooth out wrinkles. Tape edges of plastic wrap to back of cardboard. Place egg pattern on top of plastic wrap. Trace shape twice, transferring vertical markings to 1 egg and horizontal markings to remaining egg. Using craft knife, cut out each egg shape along outside edge. Then cut stacked eggs into appliqué pieces, following vertical or horizontal lines.

3 Using disappearing-ink fabric marker, transfer egg pattern to front of shirt as desired. Using paintbrush and working on a small area at at time, apply Napkin Appliqué Glue inside marked areas on sweatshirt. Mixing colors as desired, press egg pieces, 1 at a time, onto glue-covered areas (see photo). Smooth out any air bubbles. Brush

another coat of glue on top of plastic. Sprinkle glitter onto eggs while glue is still wet. Let dry.

4 Using pink dimensional paint, write "Easter Egg-stravaganza" across sweatshirt. Sprinkle glitter onto wet paint. Let dry. Referring to photo, embellish each egg with dimensional paints as desired. Let dry.

5 Do not wash shirt for at least 2 weeks. Turn shirt wrong side out, wash by hand in cold water, and hang to dry.

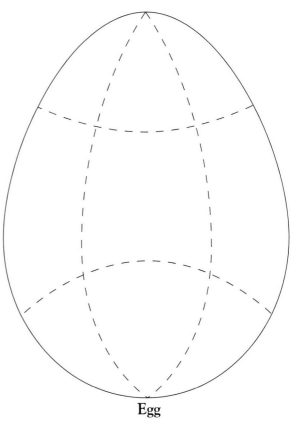

Egg

Christmas Penguin

by Barbara Spring
Park Forest, Illinois

"Penguins fascinate me and always bring a smile to my face," says Barbara Spring. "They're sort of like the puppies of Christmas. When I designed this project, I knew I wanted to create a penguin that wasn't made from felt or pom-poms. I browsed through my craft room and just made him from materials I had on hand."

Materials
Clear acrylic spray sealer
Paintbrushes
2"-diameter wooden ball with flat bottom
2¼" wooden oval with flat bottom and top
2½" wooden heart
Sandpaper
Aleene's Premium-Coat™ Acrylic Paints: Black, White, True Orange
Orange Sculpey III modeling compound
Aleene's Designer Tacky Glue™
Black Fun Foam
Foam-core board: 1 (¾" x 2") piece, 1 (1" x 1½") piece
Foil wrapping paper scraps: gold, red
Thin gold cording
Green yarn and size 11 knitting needles *or* 1¼" x 15" scrap fabric
Pinking shears (optional)

Directions

1 Apply sealer to wooden ball and wooden oval. Let dry. Lightly sand each. Referring to **Diagram A** and using Black and White paints, paint wooden ball for head and wooden oval for body. Paint 1 side and edge of wooden heart True Orange. Let dry. Turn heart over and paint remaining side. Let dry. Lightly coat each wooden piece with sealer. Let dry.

Diagram A

113

2 From modeling compound, make nose ½" in diameter at base and about ¾" long. Slightly curve end of nose. Press base of nose against face so that it fits curve of head. Remove nose. Let harden.

3 Referring to photo, glue wooden oval to wooden heart. Let dry. Glue wooden ball to wooden oval. Let dry. Transfer wing pattern to Fun Foam and cut 2 wings. Referring to **Diagram B,** glue top edge of wings to body. Let dry.

4 Cover ¾" x 2" piece of foam core with gold foil, wrapping as you would a package and using glue to secure. Repeat to wrap 1" x 1½" piece of foam core, using red foil. Tie each package with gold cording. Referring to photo, glue packages to each other and then to penguin body. Glue bottom edge of each wing in place, bending slightly.

5 For knitted scarf, using knitting needles and green yarn, cast on 5 stitches. Knit 10"-long scarf. Cast off. Tie lengths of yarn to short ends for fringe. For fabric scarf, cut both long edges of fabric with pinking shears. Pull a few threads to fringe each short end of fabric. Tie scarf around penguin's neck. Glue nose in place.

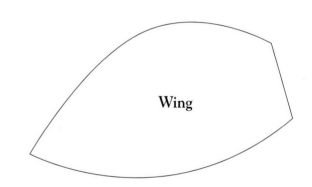

Wing

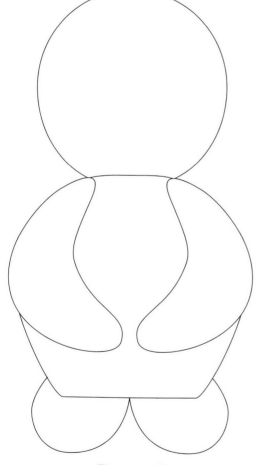

Diagram B

114

Ghost Button-Ups

by Mary A. Dusenberry
Chillicothe, Missouri

"I developed this project after seeing Heidi place flowers around the button-hole of a shirt, using Aleene's Paper Napkin Appliqué Glue," Mary Dusenberry says. "I liked the look and wondered if the decoration could be made to be removable, like a button cover. In my first experiment with Fun Foam, I fused fabric to the foam and made apple button-ups with matching earrings. I wore them to work and received rave reviews."

Materials
File folder
Embroidery scissors
White Fun Foam
Craft knife
Black dimensional craft paint with tip

Directions

1 Transfer ghost pattern to file folder and cut out, using embroidery scissors. Transfer pattern to Fun Foam as many times as desired. Cut out.

2 Using craft knife, cut slit in each ghost where indicated. Referring to photo and pattern for placement, paint eyes and mouth on each with black dimensional paint. Let dry.

3 To wear, button shirt. Slip ghost button-ups over desired buttons.

Cut slit.

Ghost

Wooden-Spoon Reindeer

by Joanne Seefeld
Saint Cloud, Florida

"Reindeer are one of my favorite Christmas characters," says Joanne Seefeld. *"So when I saw a figure made out of wooden spoons, I decided to see if I could turn those same type of spoons into a reindeer."*

Materials (for 1 reindeer)

6 wooden spoons
Brown wood stain
Paintbrushes: medium, small
Small handsaw
Aleene's Premium-Coat™ Acrylic Paint: Black
Sandpaper
Aleene's Designer Tacky Glue™
1 strip false eyelashes
2 (12-mm) eyes
Pom-poms: 1 (1/4"-diameter) red, 2 (1/2"-diameter) tan, 4 (2"-diameter) white
Felt: tan scraps, 3" x 8" piece green
12" length jute cording
Aleene's Fabric Stiffener™
Plastic wrap
2 1/4" x 6 3/4" piece Christmas print fabric
Aleene's Jewel-It™
1 yard silver pearl cording
1 small jingle bell
8" length 1/8"-wide red satin ribbon

Directions

1 Stain all spoons. Let dry. Referring to photo and using saw, trim handle of 4 spoons to point. Paint each point with Black. Let dry. Saw half-moon shape from rounded end of 1 remaining spoon for tail. Lightly sand to make smooth. Set aside. For head, saw off all but 1 1/2" of handle on remaining spoon. Using Tacky Glue, glue eyelashes to back of eyes. Glue eyes to flat back of short-handled spoon. Referring to photo, glue red pom-pom to 1 tan pom-pom; glue tan pom-pom in place for nose. Let dry.

2 Transfer ear pattern to tan felt and cut 2 ears. Cut slit in each where indicated. Overlap slit of each and glue. Let dry. Referring to photo, glue ears in place on flat back of spoon. Let dry. Soak jute in fabric stiffener. Place jute on plastic wrap. Cut and shape jute into antlers. Let dry. (To set fabric stiffener quickly, place antlers in microwave for 30 seconds.) Glue antlers to flat back of spoon behind ears. Let dry. From remaining tan felt, cut 1 piece to cover back of spoon. Glue in place. Let dry.

3 Glue 2 white pom-poms together. Set aside. For front of reindeer, referring to photo, sandwich short-handled spoon between 2 spoons with pointed ends. Place 1 white pom-pom in front of short-handled spoon between pointed-end spoons. Glue short-handled spoon and pom-pom in place. Let dry. For back of reindeer, referring to photo, sandwich wooden tail piece between 2 remaining spoons with pointed ends. Place 1 white pom-pom below tail piece between pointed-end spoons. Glue tail piece and pom-pom in place. Let dry. Referring to photo, glue remaining tan pom-pom behind tail piece. Let dry. Place 2 glued white pom-poms between sets of spoons and glue all 3 pieces together to form reindeer. Let dry.

4 For blanket, trim each short end of green felt and Christmas print fabric into curve. Center fabric on green felt and glue with Jewel-It Glue. Let dry. Using Jewel-It Glue, glue silver pearl cording around edge of Christmas print fabric. Let dry. Referring to photo and using Tacky Glue, glue blanket across middle of reindeer. Let dry. Thread jingle bell onto red ribbon. Tie ribbon in bow around reindeer's neck.

Cut slit.

Ear

Uncle Sam

by Susan W. Shamblin
Lynchburg, Virginia

"I work craft shows on the weekends and have designed many projects for sale and for my personal use," says Susan Shamblin. *"I love Americana crafts and in particular Uncle Sam. I also love chubby characters, so I decided to design a chubby Uncle Sam."*

Materials
Paper twist: peach, navy, white, red
Styrofoam balls: 2 (1"-diameter), 1 (2"-diameter)
32-gauge floral wire
Stuffing
Aleene's Tacky Glue™
Small sequin stars
White curly hair
1 small flag

Directions
1 For hands, cut 2 (4"-diameter) circles from peach paper twist. Place 1 (1"-diameter) Styrofoam ball in center of 1 paper twist circle and evenly gather paper around ball to cover. Secure with wire, leaving ¾" stem. Repeat with remaining 1"-diameter ball and peach circle. Set aside.

2 For arms, cut 2 (7½"-diameter) circles from navy paper twist. Place 1½"-diameter ball of stuffing in center of 1 paper twist circle and evenly gather paper around stuffing to cover. Secure with wire about 1" from cut edges, leaving wire slightly loose. Add more stuffing through opening to shape arm. Do not stuff too tightly. Dip stem of 1 hand into Tacky Glue. Insert hand stem into arm opening. Tighten wire. Cut narrow strip of navy paper twist and glue around arm to cover wire. Let dry. Repeat to complete second arm and hand. Set aside.

3 For head, cut 1 (9"-diameter) circle from peach paper twist. Place 2"-diameter Styrofoam ball in center of circle and evenly gather paper around ball to cover. Secure with wire, leaving 1" stem. Set aside.

4 For body, cut 1 (15"-diameter) circle from white paper twist. (You may need to glue several strips of paper twist together to get necessary dimensions.) Place handful of stuffing in center of paper twist circle and evenly gather paper around stuffing. Secure with wire about 1½" from cut edges, leaving 1" opening. Add more stuffing through opening to shape body. Stuff until fairly firm. Straighten gathers in paper twist. Dip stem of head into Tacky Glue. Insert head stem into body opening. Tighten wire. Let dry.

5 Cut 3 (½" x 15") strips from red paper twist. Spacing evenly, glue strips around body. Glue sequin stars to red strips as desired. Cut narrow strip of red paper twist and glue around neck to cover wire. Let dry. Make bow tie from navy paper twist. Glue bow tie to front neck area. Glue curly hair to top and back of head. Glue small amount of curly hair to chin for goatee. Referring to photo for placement, glue 1 arm to each side of body. Let dry. Glue flag in place, attaching to body and arm. Let dry.

6 For hat, from navy paper twist, cut 1 (2½"-diameter) circle and 1 (2" x 5½") rectangle. Cut out center of circle, leaving ½"-wide brim. Set center piece aside for later use. Overlap short ends of rectangle, making sure resulting tube will fit into opening in brim. Glue ends together. Let dry. Cut ¼" slits in both short edges of tube. Fold resulting tabs on 1 end to outside; fold tabs on opposite end to inside. Slide brim down over tube so that brim rests on tabs folded to outside. Glue brim to tabs. Glue set-aside center piece to tabs folded to inside at top of hat. Let dry. Stuff hat. Cut 1 (½" x 5") strip from red paper twist. Glue around hat, just above brim. Glue sequin stars to red hatband as desired. Glue hat to top of head. Let dry.

Gingerbread Magnets

by Cindy Shinsky
Muse, Pennsylvania

"I was visiting someone not long after Christmas and noticed that she had already thrown away her Christmas cards. This gave me the idea to make a card that people would want to keep from year to year and that could be mailed easily," says Cindy Shinsky. *"The gingerbread girl magnets were our 1995 Christmas cards. The gingerbread boys will be our 1996 cards. Now it's fun to visit and see our cards on friends' refrigerators."*

Materials (for 1 girl and 1 boy)
Darice™ Foamies: brown, red, green, black
Dimensional craft paints with tip: white, black, pink
Aleene's Tacky Glue™
Buttons: 2 white, 2 black
Self-stick magnet tape
Gold paint pen (optional)

Directions for girl
Transfer patterns here and on page 122 to foam and cut 1 body from brown, 1 bow and 1 dress from red, and 1 tree from green. Referring to photo, embellish each piece with paints. Let dry. Referring to photo, glue pieces together. Let dry. Glue 1 white button to each strap of dress. Let dry. Cut desired length of magnet. Adhere to back of girl. Write message on back of girl with gold paint pen or paints. Let dry.

Directions for boy
Transfer patterns here and on page 122 to foam and cut 1 body from brown; 1 hat from black; 1 hatband, 1 bow tie, and 1 candy cane from red; and 1 overalls from green. Referring to photo, embellish pieces with paints. Let dry.

Referring to photo, glue pieces together. Let dry. Glue 1 black button to each strap of overalls. Let dry. Cut desired length of magnet. Adhere to back of boy. Write message on back of boy with gold paint pen or paints. Let dry.

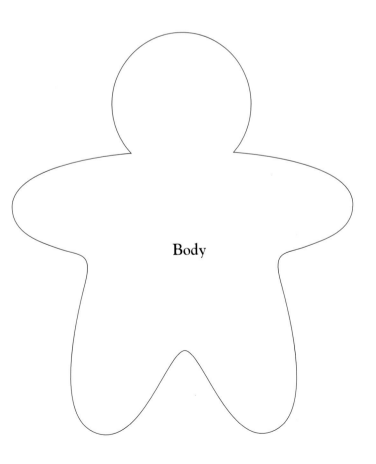

Body

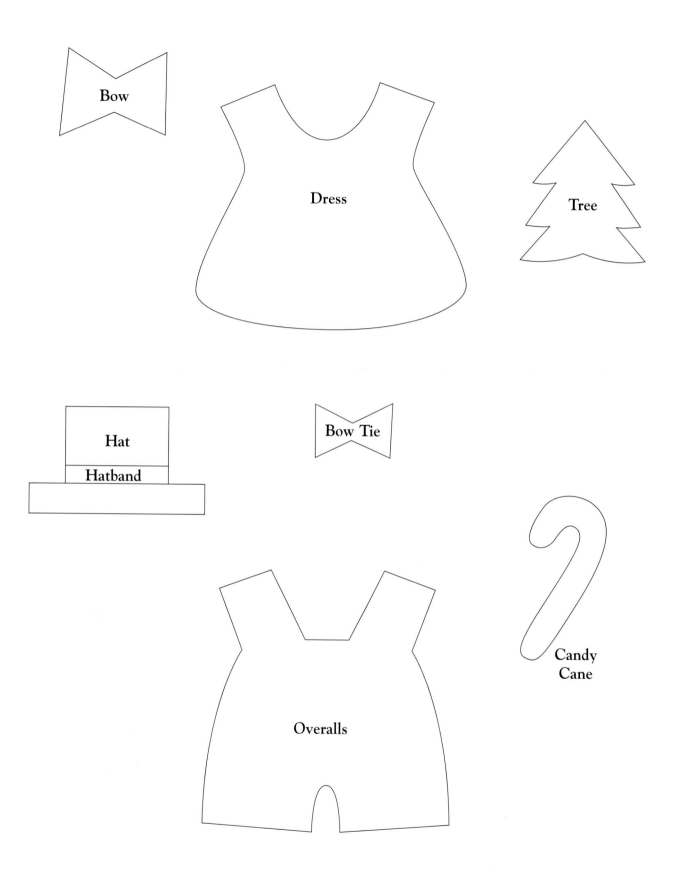

Valentine Gift Box

by Laurieann Marona
Graham, Washington

"This gift box is easy to make and very inexpensive," says Laurieann Marona. Give it by itself or fill it with goodies for a special valentine presentation.

Materials
Papier-mâché heart-shaped box
Puff paint
Gold spray paint

Directions

1 Using puff paint, paint desired designs free-hand on box base and box lid. Do not paint bottom of box or inside of lid. Let dry thoroughly.

2 Spray-paint box gold. Let dry. Apply additional coats of gold paint as needed to cover puff paint and box, letting dry between coats.

Turkey & Santa Place Mat

by Patty Clark
Centralia, Washington

"This reversible place mat came about when a friend wanted something to put out at Thanksgiving and also at Christmas," says Patty Clark. "So with leftover quilt scraps and an idea, I came up with this. Once I had drawn the turkey on a piece of paper bag, I cut it out and turned it over. From this outline, I created the Santa face."

Materials (for 1 place mat)

Fabrics: 1 yard 45"-wide muslin, ⅓ yard red print, 9" x 16" piece green print, 8" x 16" piece yellow print, 6" x 15" piece brown print, 5" square brown solid, 6" x 11" piece beige print, 5" x 7" piece pink solid, ¼ yard white fleece, blue and rose scraps

Disappearing-ink fabric marker
Plain paper
Aleene's Fusible Web™
4 (14" x 16") pieces lightweight batting
White thread
Dimensional fabric paints with tip: black, white

Once your Thanksgiving feast is complete, flip this turkey place mat over and continue to use the mat throughout the holiday season.

The top of the turkey's feathers becomes the bottom of Santa's beard.

Directions

1 From muslin, cut 4 (15" x 22") pieces. Transfer entire turkey pattern to 1 piece of muslin. Transfer entire Santa pattern to separate piece of muslin. Set muslin pieces aside.

2 Transfer individual turkey and Santa pattern pieces to paper, adding ¼" seam allowance to each piece except those noted on pattern pages. (Transfer 1 continuous strip per color for turkey tail feathers.) Cut out. Reverse patterns and transfer to paper side of fusible web. Cut out.

3 Referring to manufacturer's instructions, fuse each piece to wrong side of designated color of fabric (see photo). Cut out. Remove paper backing. Fuse turkey fabric pieces to marked muslin piece in order indicated. Repeat with Santa fabric pieces.

4 Layer muslin, batting, and turkey right side up. Using small zigzag stitch and white thread, zigzag along edges of each fused piece except eyes. Zigzag along feather lines in turkey's tail. Straightstitch close to edge along outside of entire turkey. Trim muslin and batting to within 1" of straightstitching. Stitch and trim Santa in same manner.

5 With right sides facing and edges aligned, stitch turkey and Santa together, stitching through all thicknesses and leaving smooth curved edge open. (Top of turkey wings will align with bottom of Santa's beard.) Trim seam allowance and clip curves. Turn. Press. Slipstitch opening closed. Tack layers together in unnoticeable spots. Using black paint, outline turkey and Santa eyes. Using white paint, add accent dot inside each eye. Let dry.

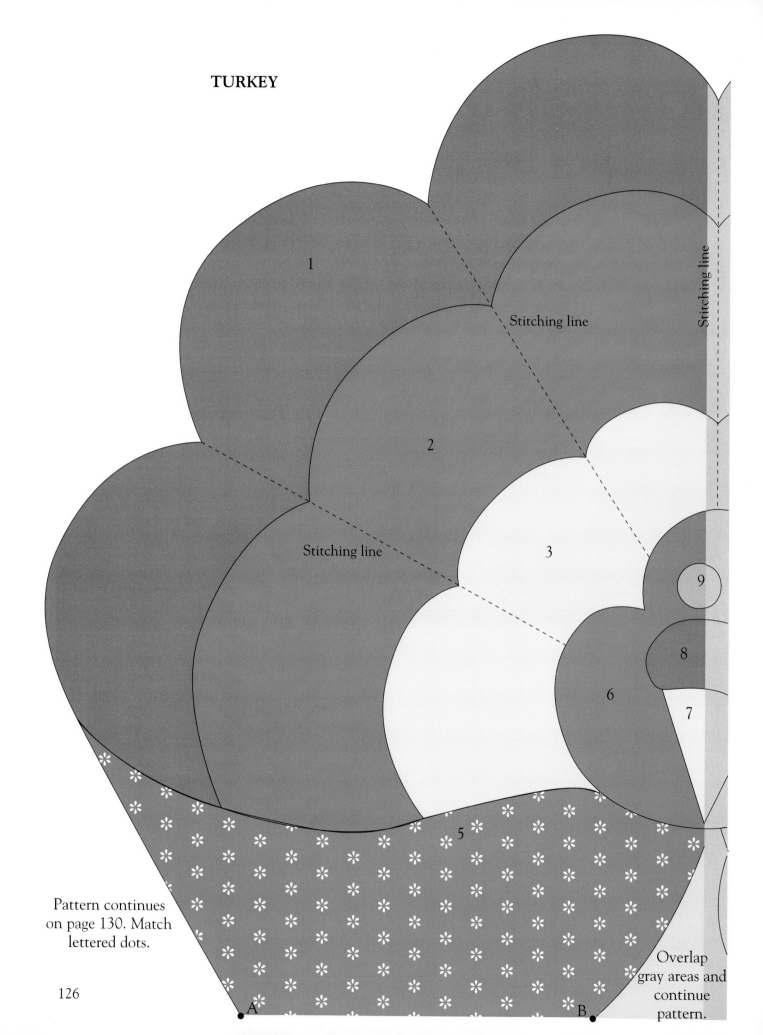

TURKEY

1

Stitching line

2

Stitching line

3

9

8

6

7

5

Pattern continues on page 130. Match lettered dots.

Stitching line

Overlap gray areas and continue pattern.

A

B

126

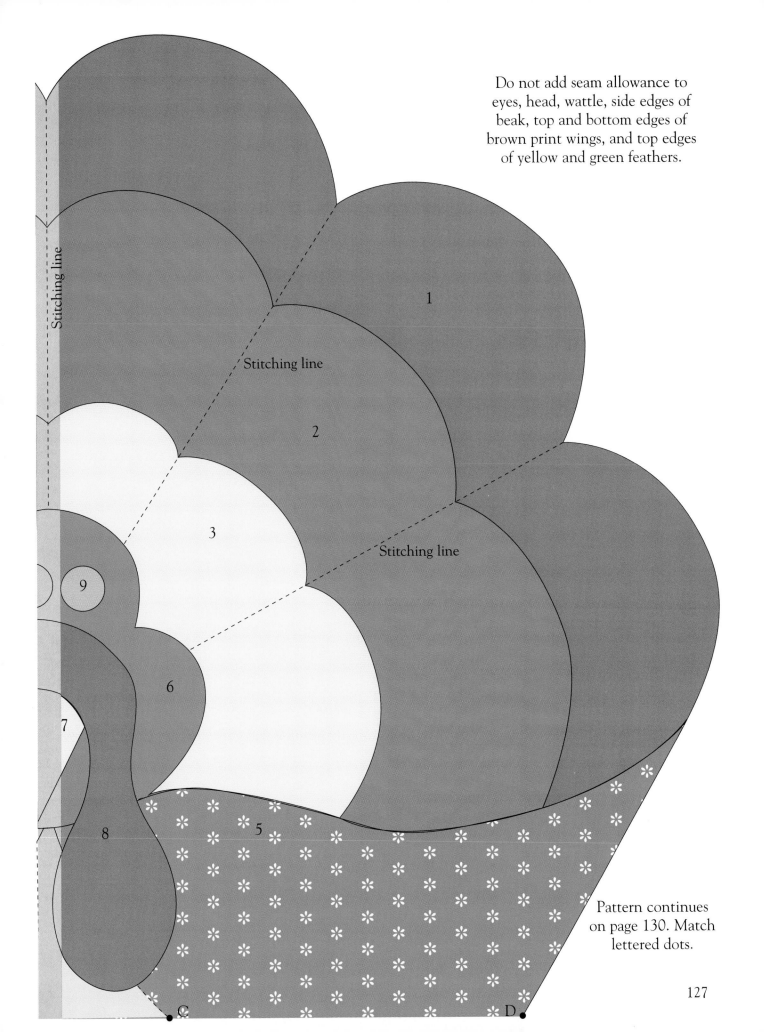

Do not add seam allowance to
eyes, head, wattle, side edges of
beak, top and bottom edges of
brown print wings, and top edges
of yellow and green feathers.

Stitching line

Stitching line

Stitching line

Stitching line

1

2

3

9

6

7

8

5

Pattern continues
on page 130. Match
lettered dots.

C

D

127

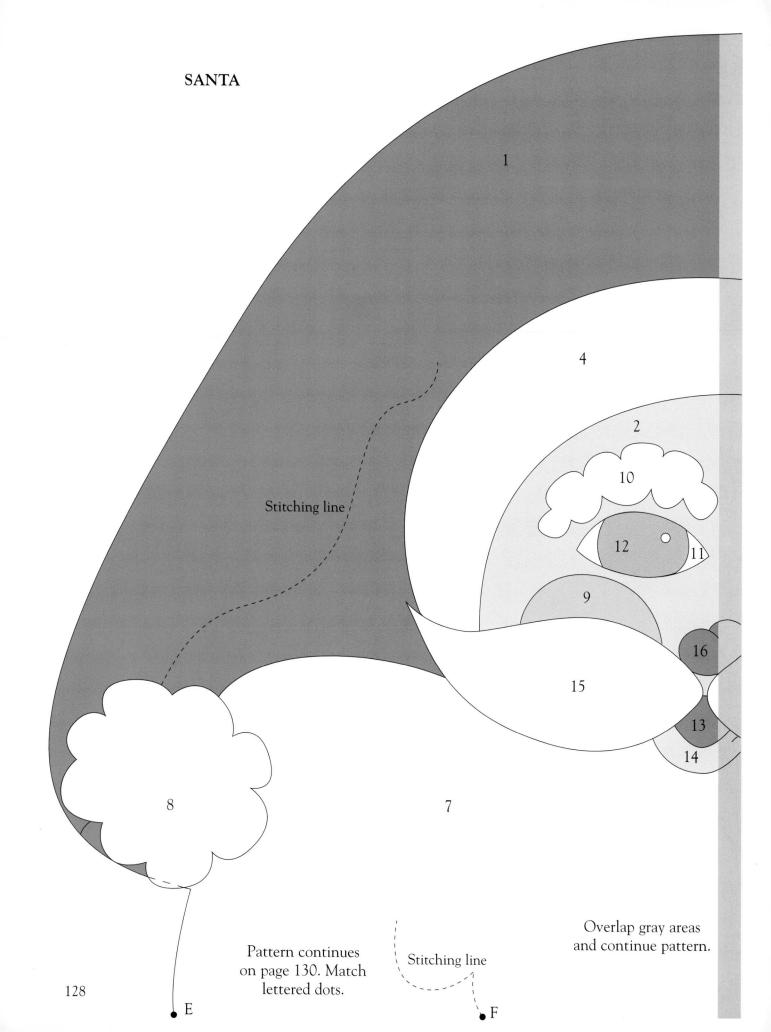

SANTA

1

Stitching line

4

2

10

12

11

9

16

15

13

14

8

7

Pattern continues
on page 130. Match
lettered dots.

Stitching line

Overlap gray areas
and continue pattern.

128

E

F

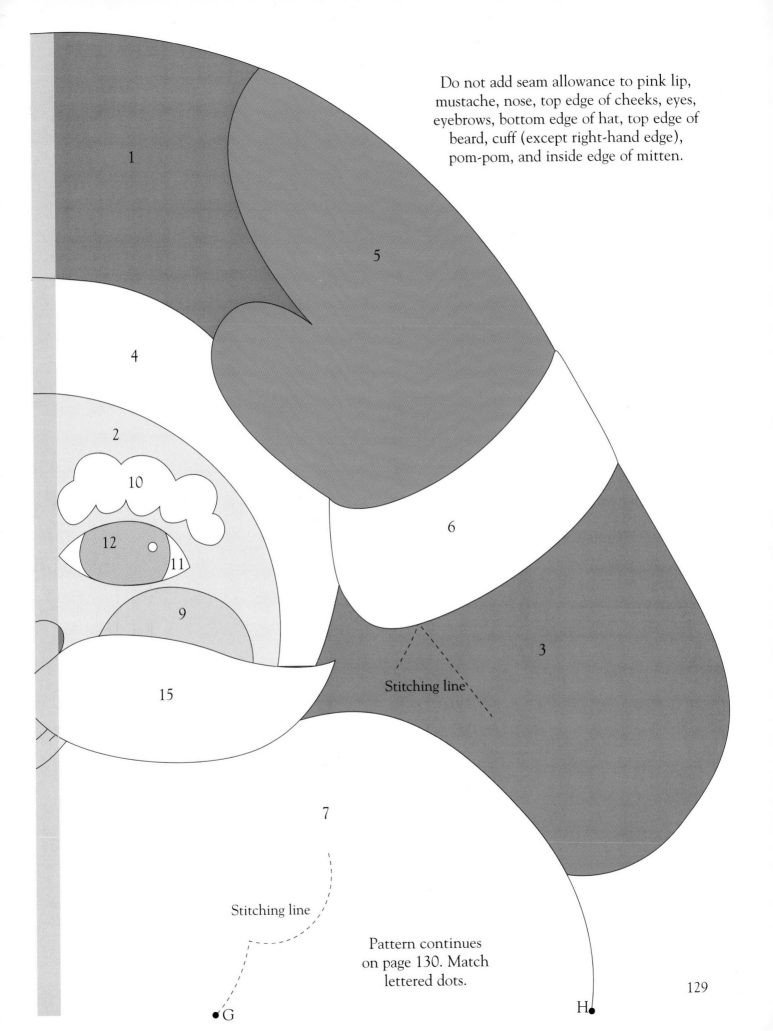

Do not add seam allowance to pink lip, mustache, nose, top edge of cheeks, eyes, eyebrows, bottom edge of hat, top edge of beard, cuff (except right-hand edge), pom-pom, and inside edge of mitten.

1

5

4

2

10

12

11

9

6

15

3

Stitching line

7

Stitching line

Pattern continues
on page 130. Match
lettered dots.

•G

H•

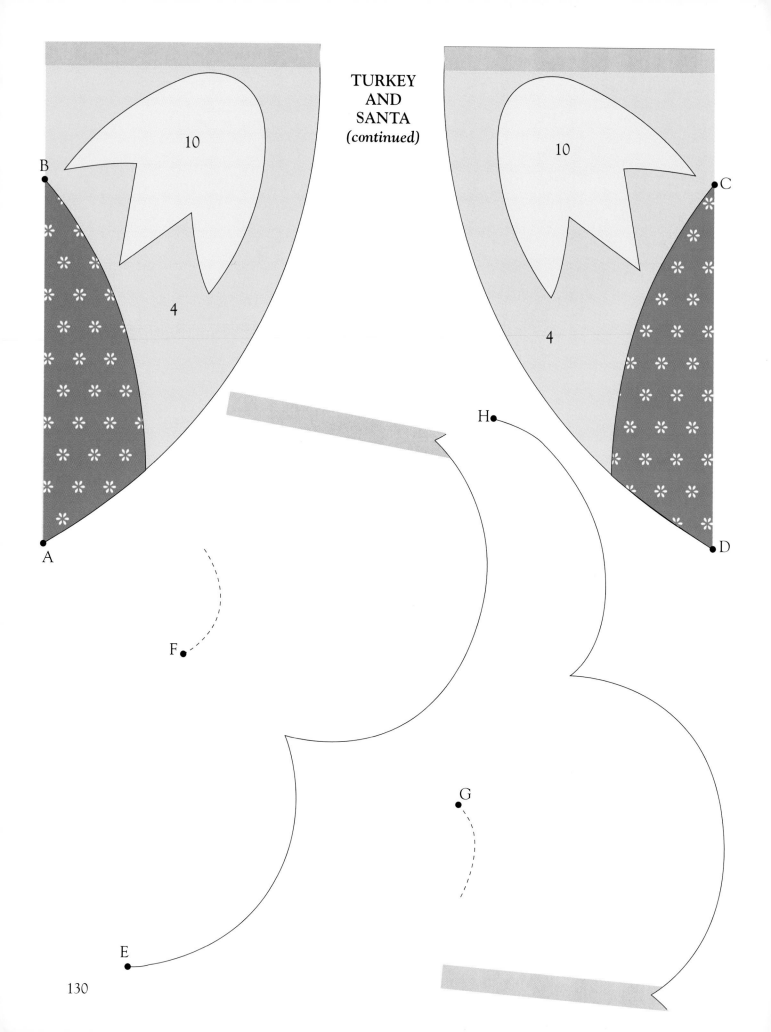

TURKEY
AND
SANTA
(continued)

B

10

4

A

C

10

4

D

H

F

G

E

Beaded Indian Corn Pin

by Kathy Bidler
Rowland Heights, California

"I've been crafting since my early teens, when my mom got me started," says Kathy Bidler. "I love to make things for the holidays, especially small pins. Now I teach my mom how to make pins, and she makes them for all her friends at the hospital where she volunteers."

Materials

1 (6-mm) beige chenille stem
Plastic grocery bag
3 (4-mm) amber transparent faceted beads
Transparent tri-beads: 13 amber, 12 each gold and brown, 3 each orange and red
Pliers
¾" pin back
Aleene's Designer Tacky Glue™

Directions

1 Cut chenille stem into thirds. Roughly cut grocery bag into 60 strips, approximately ¼" wide and 4" long.

2 Thread faceted bead onto 1 end of each chenille stem length. Using pliers, bend back each end ¼" to form corncob end.

3 Referring to **Diagram,** for right ear of corn, thread tri-beads on top of faceted bead in the following order: gold, amber, brown, and orange. Repeat 2 more times; then add 1 gold and 1 amber. In same manner, make left ear of corn, threading in the following order: brown, amber, gold, and red. Repeat 2 more times; then add 1 brown and 1 amber. Repeat for center ear of corn, threading in the following order: gold, brown, and amber. Repeat 4 more times.

4 Twist chenille stems together to connect ears of corn. For husks, place center of grocery bag strips at chenille stem twist. Fold chenille stems over tightly to attach husks to corn. Trim excess chenille stems as desired. Glue bar pin to back at base of husks. Let dry. Roughly trim ends of husks.

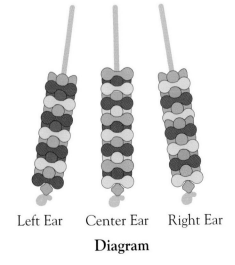

Left Ear   Center Ear   Right Ear

Diagram

Plastic
Canvas Angel

by Sheri Strunk
Perris, California

"I've always believed in angels," says Sheri Strunk. "When I began designing this project, I had no idea what it would turn out to be. I said a little prayer to help me. Then I just began playing around and, step by step, my angel earned her wings."

Materials
4" square 7 mesh plastic canvas
Craft knife
Waxed paper
Aleene's Tacky Glue™
Iridescent glitter
Aleene's Glaze-It™
Aleene's Premium-Coat™ Acrylic Paints: flesh color, Gold, Dusty Fuchsia, eye color, True Red
Paintbrush
1 round-head clothespin
1"-diameter wooden ball with hole
Wool for hair
Straight pin
1 yard gold cording
Aleene's Designer Tacky Glue™
6" length 3"-wide gold webbed ribbon
4" length pearl cording
Fine-tip permanent black marker

Directions
1 Place plastic canvas on top of template on page 134. Using craft knife, cut section from upper right corner of canvas. Place canvas on waxed paper. Squeeze layer of Tacky Glue on 1 side of canvas, filling in each hole with glue. Generously sprinkle glitter over glue-covered canvas and gently press glitter into glue with finger. Using craft knife, carefully cut around outside edges of canvas, cutting through waxed paper. Do not remove waxed paper until glue is almost dry. Then carefully remove waxed paper from back of canvas. Let dry completely. Apply 2 to 3 coats of Glaze-It, letting dry between coats.

2 Paint clothespin and wooden ball with flesh paint. Let dry. For angel's shoes, referring to photo on page 134, paint ends of clothespin Gold. Let dry. Using Tacky Glue, glue wool to wooden ball for angel's hair. Let dry.

3 Referring to template, with glitter side to outside, fold Point A to Point B and Point C to Point D to form a cone. Punch out every third hole from bottom edge up to fifteenth hole, using straight pin. From gold cording, cut 1 (20") length. Beginning at bottom hole and referring to **Diagram**, lace punched holes as though lacing a shoe. Do *not* knot ends of cording.

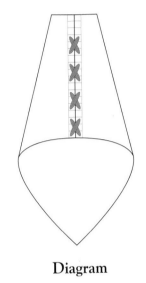

Diagram

4 Insert clothespin into folded canvas, leaving angel's shoes extending 1" beyond laced edges of canvas. Using Designer Tacky Glue, glue wooden ball to round end of clothespin. Let dry.

5 Pinch webbed ribbon in center; tie with free ends of cording from laced back. Knot cording to secure. Tie free ends of cording in bow, leaving enough for hanger (see photo). Shape ribbon to form wings. Using Tacky Glue, glue each bottom point of ribbon to back of angel. Let dry.

6 For halo, cut 1 (3½") length from gold cording. Shape into circle and glue to hair. Let dry. Using Designer Tacky Glue, glue pearl cording around neck. Let dry. For shoelaces, cut 2 (3") lengths from gold cording. Referring to photo on page 134, glue 1 end of 1 length of cording to inside of 1 leg. Crisscross cording around leg and glue remaining end to inside of leg. Let dry. Repeat to embellish remaining shoe. Referring to photo, paint features on angel's face, using marker for eyelashes, eyebrows, and pupils. Let dry. If desired, sprinkle glitter in angel's hair.

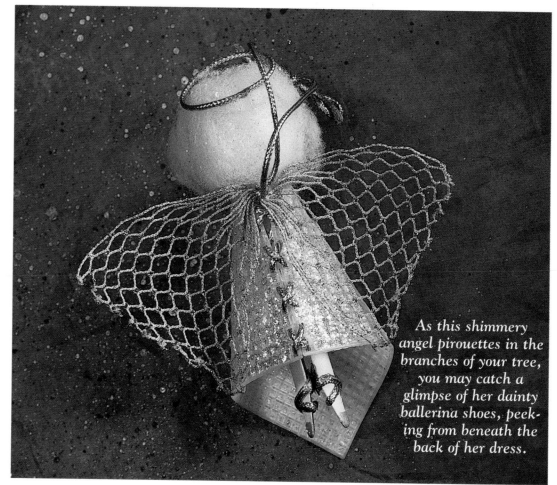

As this shimmery angel pirouettes in the branches of your tree, you may catch a glimpse of her dainty ballerina shoes, peeking from beneath the back of her dress.

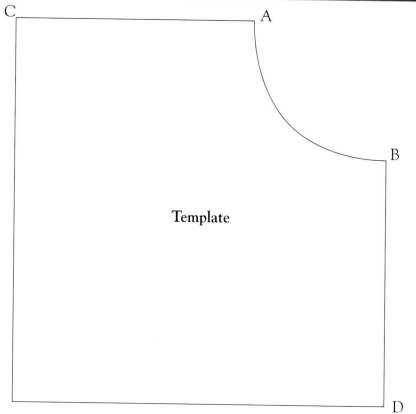

C　　　　　　　　　　A

B

Template

D

Light Bulb Ghost

by Kathleen Dolan DeWitt
Wisconsin Rapids, Wisconsin

"I had made my mother a light bulb pumpkin for Halloween and thought I should make something out of a candelabra light bulb," says Kathleen Dolan DeWitt. *"I decided it looked like a ghost. Now everyone saves burned-out light bulbs for me!"*

Materials
Candelabra light bulb
Aleene's Premium-Coat™ Acrylic Paints: Black, White
Paintbrushes
9" length black wire garland with bats
Low-temperature glue gun and glue sticks
Fine-tip permanent markers: black, red
Clear acrylic spray varnish
Black felt scraps
Aleene's Designer Tacky Glue™

Directions

1 Paint base of light bulb Black. Let dry. To make hanger, twist 1" at each end of garland together. Wrap twisted ends of garland around base of light bulb and, using glue gun, glue in place. Let dry.

2 Apply 2 to 3 coats of White paint to light bulb, letting paint dry between coats. Referring to photo, use markers to draw ghost's features. Spray entire bulb with varnish. Let dry.

3 Transfer hat and brim patterns to black felt and cut 1 of each. Cut X in brim as indicated on pattern. Referring to photo, slip brim over base of light bulb. Wrap hat around base of light bulb, overlap ends, and glue, using Tacky Glue. Let dry.

Hat

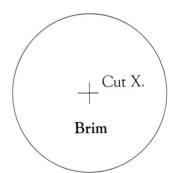

+ Cut X.

Brim

135

Bread Dough Bridal Veil

by Cindy Paffhausen
Butte, Montana

"I sew formalwear for weddings and proms, and I make bridal veils," says Cindy Paffhausen. *"A floral spray I was using recently to accent a veil had some clear plastic flowers on it. When I saw the flowers, it occurred to me that bread dough roses would also look great on a veil."*

Materials
2 slices white bread with crust removed
Plastic cup
Aleene's Tacky Glue™
Craft stick
Aleene's Premium-Coat™ Acrylic Paint: White
Zip-top plastic bag
Straight pin
Aleene's Designer Tacky Glue™
White fabric-covered barrette
Pearl acrylic craft paint
Small paintbrush
Clear gloss sealer
Tulle
Rotary cutter with wavy blade and mat

Directions

1 Referring to box on page 31, make bread dough recipe, using 2 tablespoons of Aleene's Tacky Glue and White paint in center well.

2 To make each rose, pinch off pea-sized bit of dough. Squeeze pea between fingers to flatten into small round piece the thickness of paper. For center of rose, roll flattened piece, turning top edge back slightly to look as if rose were just beginning to unfurl. Pinch off another pea-sized piece of dough and flatten as before. Press top edge back slightly to make petal. Wrap petal around center, gently pressing together at bottom. Make next petal and place opposite first petal; press together at bottom.

Continue in same manner to add total of 10 petals, overlapping edges slightly and placing subsequent petals higher on rose so that turned-back edges are even with rose center. Cut off bottom of rose before it dries completely. Let dry. Repeat to make as many roses in various sizes as desired.

3 To make each leaf, pinch off pea-sized piece of dough and mold into teardrop shape. Flatten teardrop so that it is a bit thicker than paper. Using straight pin, make indentions in top of leaf for veins. Curl leaf as desired. Let dry. Repeat to make as many leaves as desired.

4 Using Designer Tacky Glue and referring to photo, glue roses and leaves to barrette as desired. Let dry. Paint roses and leaves, using pearl paint. Let dry. Apply coat of gloss sealer. Let dry.

5 Cut tulle to desired length and in desired number of layers. Trim edges, using rotary cutter with wavy blade. Gather top edges of tulle to width of barrette and secure.

6 Using Designer Tacky Glue, glue tulle to back of barrette along bottom edge. Let dry.

Thanksgiving Dinner Bell

by Stephanie Kay Lewis
Bountiful, Utah